One Nation Under God

A trial lawyer exposes the myth of the
separation between church & state

Dee Wampler

Evergreen
PRESS

Mobile, Alabama

One Nation Under God by Dee Wampler

Copyright © 2008 Dee Wampler

All rights reserved. This book is protected under the copyright laws of the United States of America. This book may not be copied or reprinted for commercial gain or profit.

ISBN 978-1-58169-284-6

For Worldwide Distribution

Printed in India.

Evergreen Press

P.O. Box 191540 • Mobile, AL 36619

800-367-8203

Table of Contents

PART ONE: THE PAST

PART TWO: THE PRESENT

PART THREE: THE FUTURE

Foreword

The United States of America is a country founded by men of God who expressed their belief in a divine Creator in virtually every major document they penned. God and church were a part and parcel of the American way of life. What was so evident then has become a major issue of contention now. A small minority are driving God and church out of the American culture whenever and wherever they can.

Conservative Americans who oppose abortion, homosexuality, same sex marriage, and pornography find themselves on the defensive. Christians are pictured as narrow-minded, uncaring individuals who have no compassion. To win the battles, Christians must move from standing in defensive positions to taking offensive ones. We must switch the debate. The God of the Bible must be made the issue.

We are at a critical point in the history of our country. Two religious perspectives stand in stark contrast with each other, both desiring that their religion serve as the basis of our values. Islam and the Judeo-Christian faiths are now clashing because adherents of both want their beliefs to serve as the foundation of our cultural values. There is a vast difference between these two value systems. One wants forced submission to Allah achieved by the sword; the other desires voluntary submission to God achieved by a changed heart. Perhaps this clash of value systems will force us to re-examine our core principles if our system of democracy is to continue.[1]

Beyond the influence of the Islamic faith are the atheists who want to remove any mention of God from our society today. These people have been successful in removing prayer from our schools, but that was only the beginning of their agenda. A vocal minority of the American public refuses to acknowledge our Christian heritage. These heritage-deniers are powerful people who run universities and public schools, hold high public office, wear black robes, and decide what is broadcast on the news and printed in the newspaper. Some are merely ignorant of what contemporary Americans of faith believe and how they live their lives, and some are openly hostile to those beliefs—and paranoid. They cannot imagine that the Founding Fathers, those brilliant architects of our democracy, were Americans of great faith.

Throughout history nations have built monuments, usually to record victories in battle or to honor their gods. Every nation's monuments and national symbols reflect the heart of the people and identify what they believe is the apex of their nation's achievements. Unlike most nations, America's monuments were not built to record countries conquered or battles won. America's memorials contain the declaration that the source of our birth, liberty, and greatness is God. A tour of our historic sites reveals that America was a nation birthed by men who had a firm reliance upon Almighty God and His Son Jesus Christ. Inscribed upon our buildings, monuments, and national symbols is our nation's faith in God.[2]

I pray that God will use this book to encourage Christians to take action. While

Christians do not seem to be tongue-tied when it comes to family values, they somehow become summer soldiers and sunshine patriots when it comes to government and politics.

We are lectured:

- "You can't speak out on abortion, homosexuality, pornography, gambling, prostitution; those are political issues."
- "You can't mention Christ in the public square; that's religion."
- "You can't speak about carrying out the Great Commission; that's hate speech."

Too many Christians shut their mouths, drop their weapons, and walk away. And remember, there's to be no greeting others with "Merry Christmas!" You may hurt someone's feelings. Well, don't you believe it!

I was raised in a small Midwestern town, founded on conservative principles. Hard work, honesty, and respect for God and country were taught in all public schools. We pledged allegiance to the flag and even prayed in the public school. We joined scout organizations that met in schools. Movies, television, and radio reflected patriotism; and our children and grandchildren were taught the truth of our forefathers.

Then came legalized abortion, pornography, sodomy, and the ERA mentality that mothers should become employed; the Ten Commandments and prayer were out; sex education and condoms were in. Schools now shy away from meaningful mention of our early Christian history.

In recent years our local school board deleted Christmas from its calendar. Members of the community, with the support of Gannett Corporation, spouted the "Good Community" principles and concluded that church, faith in God, the Bible, religion, or the Ten Commandments *did not qualify* as even one of the top local values. Teachers who posted the Ten Commandments were fired. In a nearby town a Wicca sued the city and won thousands of dollars because the city seal contained a tiny ichthus (sign of the fish and early Christian symbol).

Multiculturalism, liberalism, and a watering down of our local and national religious heritage have occurred in my lifetime. Our woeful neglect of America's Christian heritage is never more apparent than in the scripted history that is carefully offered on the altar of political correctness.

We have, over the course of our history, thrown out a great deal of acquired wisdom in the process of replacing it with the next new thing. Religion may no longer define the ideal world as it did for the Puritans, *but the United States is still a deeply religious society. Our language, institutions, and government reflect that heritage.*

We do, after all, have a proud history—so let's start at the beginning.

Dee Wampler
July 4, 2008

PART ONE
THE PAST

Chapter One

In the Beginning

We all want to know how it was in the beginning. From the Big Bang to the Garden of Eden, to the circumstances of our own births, we would like to travel to a time when everything was new and history was being made.

Our country's history began back in the 15th century, when a man named Cristoforo Colombo had a vision of exploring the seas and travelling to the Indies. He was positive that God was directing his path.

Christopher Columbus

Christopher Columbus was an extraordinary mariner and one of the world's most

important explorers. Until recently, he has enjoyed a prominent place in American history. Because of the historical revisionism of the Western civilization, Columbus has now become a fashionable target of ridicule. The elite like to paint Columbus as nothing more than someone who spread disease, inflicted genocide, and destroyed the native civilizations of the New World.

As you can see in Columbus' writings below, in reality he was a man who followed God and saw miracles happen before his eyes as he opened up the New World for Christianity. He was a man who saw his voyage as one that he was not only permitted to make but also inspired by God to take.

Columbus sailed August 3, 1492 with the Nina, Pinta, and Santa Maria, arriving at the Canaries and San Salvadore (Bahamas), and later sailed to Cuba and Santo Domingo (Hispaniola). When informing the Pope of Columbus' expedition to the Indies, Queen Isabella (1450–1504), Queen of Castile, wife of King Ferdinand of Aragon, and financier of Columbus' expedition, said the mission was **"To bear the light of Christ west to the heathen undiscovered lands."**

Look at the actual words of Columbus:[1]

Sunday, 23 September 1492
"The crew is still grumbling about the wind.... Later, when the sea rose up without wind, they were astonished at this sign. **I saw this as God, and it was very helpful to me. Such a sign has not appeared since Moses led the Jews out of Egypt, and they, because of this sign, did not lay violent hands on me. God used this miracle to inspire my life.**"

Thursday, 11 October 1492
"As is our custom, vespers were said in the late afternoon, and a **special thanksgiving was offered to God for giving us renewed hope** through the many signs of land He has provided.

"Then, at two hours after midnight, the Pinta fired a cannon, my prearranged signal for the sighting of land. **I now believe that the light I saw earlier was a sign from God** and that it was truly the first positive indication of land. I hauled in all sails but the mainsail and lay-to till daylight. At dawn ... I went ashore in a small boat.... **After a prayer of thanksgiving** I ordered the captains of the Pinta and Nina to record and bear witness to the act of laying claim to this land in the name of Spain. **To this island I gave the name San Salvador, in honor of our Blessed Lord.**"[2]

Wednesday, 12 December 1492
"I placed a large cross at the entrance to the harbor, on a little rise on the western side. **This is a sign that Your Highnesses possess this land as your own**

and especially as an emblem of Jesus Christ, Our Lord, and in honor of Christianity. After erecting the cross, three sailors started up the mountain to see the trees and plants.³

"Your Highnesses must be greatly pleased **because you will soon make them Christians** and will teach them the good customs of your realms, for there cannot be a better people or country.⁴ My navigation has been very accurate and I have steered well, for which **many thanks should be given to Our Lord**."⁵

Columbus also wrote in his diary, "It was the Lord who put into my mind (I could feel His hand upon me) the fact that it would be possible to sail from here to the Indies. All who heard of my project rejected it with laughter, ridiculing me.

"There is no question that the inspiration was from the Holy Spirit, because He comforted me with rays of marvelous illumination from the Holy Scriptures, a strong and clear testimony ... encouraging me continually to press forward, and without ceasing for a moment they now encourage me to make haste.

"Our Lord Jesus desired to perform a very obvious miracle in the voyage to the Indies, to comfort me and the whole people of God."

Two Hundred Years Later

It took both religious and political persecution to motivate British colonists to leave the security of civilization two centuries later and embark on a mission to carve a Christian commonwealth out of the unknown and hostile wilderness Columbus had discovered.

The purpose of the New England colonies was, with respect to church and state, twofold. First, it was to establish the true and free church, free from the control of the state so that its members could be co-workers to establish God's kingdom on earth. Second, it was to establish godly magistrates, i.e., a Christian state, with magistrates as ordained by God. The separation of Christianity from the workings of the State was not the objective of these early settlers. In fact, Christianity was the motivating force behind our founders' desire to establish a "city on a hill."⁶

Our nation began, not in 1776, but more than 160 years earlier in a small outpost called Jamestown (1607). The original Charter acknowledged the "**providence of Almighty God**" and "the glory of His Divine Majesty" to bring the "**Christian religion to (those) ... as yet live in darkness and miserable ignorance of the true knowledge and worship of God.**"

Armed with the king's commission, three ships—the Discovery, the Godspeed, and the Susan Constant—along with 144 men led by Captain Christopher Newport, left London in December 1606.⁷

The men who founded Jamestown in Virginia in 1607 were Anglican. Even though they had commerce uppermost in their minds, an Englishman's life during this time was a life suffused with God and faith. Even Captain John Smith, the mercenary, a hard-bitten hero of the colony's early years, attributed the survival of Jamestown not to the efforts of men but to the will of God.

Virginia may have been a chartered company created to bring profit to its shareholders, but the settlers nonetheless viewed reality through the prism of seventeenth-century Anglicanism.[8] This era was undergirded by religious mores. The people considered their destiny in God's hands and felt they should thank Him for their success.

The Mayflower Compact

Unfortunately, the founding of Jamestown in 1607 could hardly have been counted as a success. During the first year, 70 of the 108 settlers had died. When explaining how rescue ships from England arrived just in time to save the colony during the "starving times" (1609), Smith wrote, "the God that heard Jonah crying in the belly of hell, pitied the distress of his servants … **This was** … **the direct line of God's providence.**"

The Mayflower Compact

A little more than a decade later, a group of Christians called Separatists, who had left the Church of England, sailed on the Mayflower ship for the New World. Arguments for and against immigrating to America had ended for many with a conviction that God wanted them to make the journey. And as all God-fearing English Puritans believed, their country had been earmarked by the Lord to lead His forces in triumph. Richard Hakluyk, their chronicler and a British explorer, explained their spiritual duty to plant a godly English plantation in the new world. "We verily believe and trust the Lord is with us, and that He will graciously prosper our endeavors according to the simplicity of our hearts, therein."[9]

The Mayflower dropped anchor in the Cape Cod area of Massachusetts in November

1620. The passengers aboard the ship were suffering from malnutrition and scurvy and did not have the strength to re-embark for Virginia where they had been given a Charter for land. Because their original Charter did not apply to their new landing site, a workable governing document had to be hastily drawn up in order to avoid anarchy. On board ship they signed what we now call the Mayflower Compact—a covenant that bound

them together to obey whatever laws they might jointly pass. The group, in the words of their future governor, William Bradford, **"fell on their knees and blessed the God of Heaven who had brought them over the vast and furious ocean and delivered them** from all the perils and mysteries thereof."

The Compact reads in part:

"In the name of God, Amen. We whose names are underwritten, the loyal subjects of our dread sovereign lord King James, by the grace of God, of Great Britain, France, and Ireland, king, defender of the faith, etc., **having undertaken for the glory of God and advancement of the Christian faith,** and the honor of our king and country, a voyage to plant the first colony in the northern parts of Virginia; do by these presents, solemnly and mutually **in the presence of God** and one another covenant and combine ourselves together into a civil body politic, for our better ordering and preservation and furtherance of other ends aforesaid; and by virtue hereof do enact, constitute and frame such just and equal laws, ordinances, acts, constitutions and offices, from time to time, as shall be thought most (suitable) and convenient for the general good of the colony; unto which we promise all due submission and obedience."

The group soon moved up the coast to Plymouth and constructed ramshackle houses. The Pilgrims arrived too late in the year to plant any seed. They suffered during their first winter, with half of the colony perishing. The rest survived with the assistance from local Indians, especially one named Squanto—"a spetial instrument sent from God," as Bradford called him. For all this they gave thanks to God, establishing what would become a national tradition.

William Bradford described the colony in his *History of Plymouth Plantation:*

"They had a great hope and inward zeal of laying some good foundation, or at least to make some way thereunto, for ... "the propagating and advancing the

Gospel of the Kingdom of Christ in those remote parts of the world; yea, though they should be but even as stepping stones unto others for the performing of so great a work." Being thus arrived in a good harbor and brought safe to land, they fell upon their knees and blessed the God of heaven."

William Bradford

The Plymouth colony persisted, infused with Pilgrim piety, for seventy more years. Governor Bradford described a community that never ceased to struggle for financial security and that narrowly avoided being absorbed into the more powerful Puritan colony of Massachusetts Bay. Yet, in spite of, or perhaps because of these challenges, the Pilgrims never ceased to believe that all that mattered was the doing of God's will, and they felt certain they were setting a noble example. "As one small candle may light a thousand," Bradford wrote, "so the light kindled here hath shone to many, yea in some sort to our whole nation."[10]

Their voyage was "for the glory of God and advancement of the Christian faith." The Pilgrims understood that all of life was under the sovereign dominion of God. They believed that all their pursuits, including the building of homes, churches, and schools and carving out new homes in the wilderness, ultimately would lead to the glory of God.

Massachusetts Bay Colony

John Winthrop, the future governor of Massachusetts Bay, was caught up in the beginnings of the new nation. Little about his background suggested such an auspicious future. He owned a small manor in Suffolk and dabbled in law. But the core of Winthrop's life was his faith in God, a faith so intense his contemporaries immediately identified him as a Puritan. The Lord, he concluded, was displeased with England. In May 1629, he wrote his wife, "I am verily persuaded God will bring some heavye affliction upon this lande, and that speedylye." He was, however, confident that the Lord would "provide a shelter and a hidinge place for us."

Heading to New England on the Arbella, Winthrop and his fellow Puritans felt they were on an errand. They wanted nothing less than to construct a godly paradise:

"Hayle holy-land, wherein our holy Lord hath planted His most true and Holy Word ... me thinks I heare the Lambe of God thus speak. Come my deare little flocke, who for my sake have lefte your Country, dearest friends, and goods, and hazarded your lives o'er the rageing floods, possess this Country ... 'beware of Satan's wylye baites. He lurkes amongst you. Cunningly he waits.'

"The end is to improve our lives to do more service to the Lord, the comfort and increase of the body of Christ ... that ourselves and posterity may be the better preserved from the Common corruptions of this evil world, to serve our Lord and work out our salvation ... We are entered into Covenant with Him for this work ... Now if the Lord shall please hear us, and bring us in peace to the place we desire, then hath He ratified this Covenant" (paraphrased).

The Winthrop fleet departed England in March 1630. By the end of the first year, almost 2,000 people had arrived in Massachusetts Bay, and before the "Great Migration" concluded in the early 1640s, more than 16,000 men and women had arrived in the new Puritan colony.[11]

These particular settlers possessed a source of great strength and stability because they were bound together by a common sense of purpose. God, they insisted, had formed a special covenant with the people of Massachusetts Bay. If they fulfilled their side of the bargain, the settlers could anticipate peace and prosperity as a beacon for the rest of the Christian world. No one, not even the lowliest servant, was excused from this divine covenant, for as Winthrop stated, "Wee must be knitt together in this worke as one man." Many people throughout the ages have espoused such communal rhetoric, but these particular men and women went about the business of forming a new colony as if they truly intended to transform a religious vision into social reality.

Winthrop saw the colony as a city upon a hill and wrote the following in 1630:

City Upon a Hill

"Now the onely way to avoyde this shipwracke and to provide for our posterity is to followe the Counsell of Micah, to doe Justly, to love mercy, to walke humbly with our God, for this end, wee must be knitt together in this worke as one man, wee must entertaine each other in brotherly Affeccion, wee must be willing to abridge our selves of our superfluities, for the supply of others necessities, wee must uphold a familiar Commerce together in all meekenes, gentleness, patience and liberality, wee must delight in eache other, make others Condicions our owne, rejoice together, mourne together, labour, and suffer together, allwayes having before our eyes our Commission and Community in the worke, our Community as members of the same body, soe shall wee keepe the unitie of the spirit in the bond of peace, the Lord will be our God and delight to dwell among us, as his owne people and will command a blessing upon us in all our wayes, soe that wee shall see much more of his wisdome power goodness and truthe then formerly wee have beene acquainted with, wee shall finde that the God of Israell is among us, when tenn of us shall be able to resist a thousand of our enemies, when hee shall make us a prayse and glory, that men shall say of succeeding plantacions: the lord make it like that of New England: **for wee must Consider that wee shall be as a Citty upon a Hill, the eyes of all people are upon us; soe that if wee shall deale falsely with our god in this worke wee have undertaken and soe cause him to withdrawe his present help from us, we shall be made a story and a byword through the world**, wee shall open the mouthes of enemies to speake evill of the wayes of god and all professours for Gods sake; wee shall shame the faces of many of gods worthy servants, and cause theire prayers to be turned into Cursses upon us till wee be consumed out of the good land whether wee are going: And to shutt upp this discourse with that exhortacion of Moses that faithfull servant of the Lord in his last farewell to Israell Deut. 30. Beloved there is now sett before us life, and good, deathe and evill in that wee are Commaunded this day to love the Lord our God, and to love one another to walke in his wayes and to keepe his Commaundements and his Ordinance, and his lawes, and the Articles of our Covenant with him that wee may live and be multiplied, and that the Lord our God may blesse us in the land whether we goe to possesse it: But if our heartes shall turne away soe that wee will not obey, but shall be seduced and worship other Gods, our pleasures, and proffitts, and serve them, it is propounded unto us this day, wee shall surely perishe out of the good Land whether wee passé over this vast Sea to possesse it;

"Therefore lett us choose life, that wee, and our Seede may live; by obeyeing his voyce, and cleaveing to him, for hee is our life, and our prosperity."

John Winthrop emerged as one of the guiding lights of the colony. Strong-willed and stern, he epitomized the Puritan spirit. Recognizing that people are weak and easily tempted, his mandate was to construct a community that worked as one unit toward salvation. He believed that only God could save souls; salvation was a mystery bestowed by His grace; and upright behavior, or what the Puritans called sanctity, could be tested and observed. Winthrop saw the Puritans' task was to make sure the people in this new world acted in a sanctified manner.[12]

A measure of religious toleration developed. Underlying presuppositions about religious freedom were narrowly focused on Christians and, in most colonies, usually Protestants.

Had the colonists ever anticipated that Jews, Muslims, Buddhists, Hindus, or members of other non-Christian groups would contribute even a small minority in their region, even the most fiercely independent Protestants would have agreed to the establishment of a state church, as Massachusetts did from 1630-1830.[13]

Later outposts followed a similar path. The Fundamental Orders of Connecticut (1639) reads that "there should be an **orderly and decent government established according to God**, to order and dispose of the affairs of all the people at all seasons as occasions shall require….[T]o **maintain and preserve the liberty and purity of the Gospel of our Lord Jesus** which we now profess, as also the discipline of the churches, which, according to the truth of the said Gospel is now practiced among us.[14]

John Winthrop

The New England Confederation (1643) reads:

"Whereas we all came into these parts of America with one and the same end and aim, namely, to advance the Kingdom of our Lord Jesus Christ and to enjoy the liberties of the Gospel in purity with peace; and whereas in our settling (by a wise providence of God) we are further dispersed upon the sea coasts and rivers than was at first intended."[15]

Early Leaders

The overwhelming majority of our early leaders were strongly and openly religious.[16] There are many today who dispute this fact. Rather than acknowledge that Christianity played an important role in the formation of this nation, they instead claim just the opposite.

For example, one prominent historian amazingly asserts, "The Founding Fathers were at most deists."[17] In an article entitled, "America's Unchristian Beginning," the writer forcefully claims that "The early presidents and patriots were generally deists or Unitarians, believing in some form of impersonal Providence but rejecting the divinity of Jesus and the relevance of the Bible."[18] Another author similarly charges, "[M]ost of our other patriarchs were at best deists, (not) believing in . . . the God of the Old and New Testaments."[19] And the title of one book, *The Godless Constitution*, seems to say it all.[20]

In the 19th and 20th centuries, charges of the non-religious nature of our Founders were immediately dismissed because citizens knew about our individual Founders. That is no longer the case. The reason that such absurd accusations often go unrefuted by the average citizen is that most Americans today know very little about the true beliefs of our Founding Fathers.

The facts show that this country was founded by a society overwhelmingly Christian. By 1776, 150 years after the Christian Pilgrims first arrived on the Mayflower, 98 percent of the people in America professed to be Protestant Christians, 1.8 percent were Roman Catholic Christians, and 0.2 percent were Jewish. That means that 99.8 percent of the people in America still professed to be Christians by 1776. This country was founded by an overwhelming percentage of Christians, but of course all you hear about are the few that weren't.

If we examine the Founders, we find their ranks so replete with Bible-believing Christians as to suggest that America **at the epoch of its founding was a country awash in religious fervor** . . . .[21]

For example, the famous patriot Patrick Henry said, "**America was not founded by religionists but by Christians.** It was not founded upon religions but **upon the gospel of Jesus Christ.**"

The quest for perfection has been a hallmark of American culture since a group of settlers embarked from the old world to create a city on a hill. They did not succeed, but they made a compelling start.[22]

Chapter 2

Spiritual Foundations

The Pilgrims did not walk around in wide-brimmed hats and buckle shoes spouting platitutdes, nor does their story end with the first Thanksgiving.[1] The Great Migration of English Puritans worked hard to transform New England from a modest outpost into a complex and thriving society with settlers sharing the vision of their City on a Hill.

Except for work, religion was the most important aspect of colonial life. It was a crucial element even in limited periods of relaxation. Religion provided the community with a sense of purpose, was socially desirable, and still provided the best explanation of the world. The bonus was that it gave people the hope of an afterlife.

Officially or unofficially, most colonies had an established church and levied tithes for the support of a congregational minister. The Massachusetts Charter (1691) stated,

"There shall be a liberty of conscience allowed in the worship of God to all Christians, except Papist."[2]

The Church of England was established by law in Virginia in 1609, providing for compulsory church attendance. The Anglican Church was established in New York in 1693, Maryland in 1702, South Carolina in 1706, North Carolina in 1711, and Georgia in 1758. Congregational churches were introduced by the Pilgrims in Plymouth in 1620 and by the Puritans of Massachusetts Bay in 1630.

The larger denominations were Protestant: Congregationalists, Presbyterians, Quakers, Baptists, Anglicans, Lutherans, German Reformed, and Dutch Reformed. At the time of the Revolution, there were nearly 3,300 churches and congregations in America (one for approximately every 850 Americans), and a majority of the population attended church regularly.[3]

In Pennsylvania and Delaware, the Anglican Church reigned supreme. This was also the case in the establishments of North and South Carolina, Maryland, and a portion of New York. Connecticut and New Hampshire tried to exclude other religious groups. Rhode Island was the only providence in New England that did not have an established church. (Roger Williams, founder of Rhode Island (1631), assailed the whole notion of a Bible commonwealth, claiming there was no scriptural jurisdiction for it.) The legislature provided for liberty of conscience, but legislative sessions, like Virginia's, always began with prayers.[4]

In 1775, nine colonies had established churches, although the number declined as the Revolution approached. Many New England states had state-endorsed Congregationalist churches while Southern states favored Episcopalian churches.[5]

The Pilgrim's Vision for Government

We have been taught that the Pilgrims escaped to America, fleeing religious persecution, so it seems heretical to suggest otherwise. While it is true that the Pilgrims left England due to the religious persecution prior to boarding the Mayflower, William Bradford, a Mayflower Pilgrim and Governor of the Plymouth settlement, specified three more factors that more fully explains their flight to America:

Economic Scarcity: The Pilgrim community in the Netherlands (where many English families had fled to avoid persecution) felt there was no hope for their economic improvement. Although they enjoyed "the ordinances of God in their purity and the liberty of the gospel," the difficult economic situation in Holland make it almost impossible for them to remain there.

The Immoral Cultural Environment: Though the spiritual health of the Pilgrim community prospered there, the larger immoral Dutch culture threatened its long-term viability. Damage to the moral condition of Pilgrim youth was feared: "... the great licentiousness of the young people of the country, and the many temptations of the city [were leading Pilgrim youth] by evil example into dangerous courses.... So they saw their posterity would be in danger to degenerate and become corrupt."

A Desire to Evangelize: The Pilgrim vision included obedience to the Great Commission: "They cherished a great hope and inward zeal of laying good foundations, or at least of making some way towards it, for the propagation and advance of the gospel of the kingdom of Christ in the remote parts of the world...."

Religious freedom, therefore, wasn't enough. The Pilgrims also needed a civil government and a culture built on Christian principles. Restoration in America began with a clear understanding of the Pilgrims' purpose to come to this land, and then of their impact on America's succeeding generations. The truth trumps tradition. The Pilgrims journeyed to America not for the freedom to practice religion in the privacy of their homes and churches, but to establish a civil society built on the rock of biblical principles and to be a beacon for Christ in the world, thus ensuring an enduring and prosperous culture. The goal for restoring America should be nothing less.[6]

America would one day have a Commander in Chief who said, "It is the duty of all nations to acknowledge the Providence of Almighty God, to obey His will, to be grateful for His benefits, and humbly to implore His protection and favor."

America would have a Congress which issued a "Proclamation for a Day of Public Thanksgiving and prayer," recommending that citizens "... confess our unworthiness of the least of his favours, and to offer our fervent supplications to the God of all grace ... to cause the knowledge of Christianity to spread over all the earth."

America would have a Supreme Court which stated, "From the discovery of this

continent to the present hour, there is a single voice making this affirmation ... that this is a Christian nation.... We find everywhere a clear recognition of the same truth."

Imagine the reaction of the Establishment if any of these statements were made by today's political leaders.

Giving God All the Glory

In *A History of the English-Speaking Peoples,* Winston Churchill called the Mayflower Compact, "one of the remarkable documents in history." Paul Johnson, author of *A History of the American People,* points out the Mayflower Compact was "the single most important formative event in early American history, which would ultimately have an important bearing on the crisis of the American Republic."[7] In *Of Plymouth Plantation*, William Bradford summarizes the whole Pilgrim adventure, giving God all the glory:

Captain John Smith

Thus out of small beginnings greater things have been produced by His hand that made all things of nothing, and gives being to all things that are; and, as one small candle may light a thousand, so the light here kindled hath shown unto many, yeah in some sort to our whole nation; **let the glorious name of Jehovah have all the praise**.[8]

Captain John Smith, founder of Virginia, said that it is the duty of all Virginians to:

... **preach, baptize, into the Christian religion and by the propagation of the Gospel** to recover out of the arms of the devil, a number of poor and miserable souls wrapped up unto death in almost invincible ignorance.

The Puritans of New England, the Catholics of Maryland, and the first Virginia settlers, were extremely religious with a desire to Christianize Indians and fashion Christian societies in the New World wilderness.

In 1682, William Penn said:

God will plan America and it shall have its day ... the fifth kingdom for Glorious of Christ … may have the last part of the world, the setting of the Sun or western world to shine in.

Other signs of a strong religious presence in the early settlements are:

- Early Americans at Jamestown constructed a small chapel and 50 years later were still continuing the church tradition by levying taxes and ordering settlers to pay ministers.
- Maryland enacted legislation in 1692 which established the Church of England and collected taxes to manage parish business.
- In 1693, New York (including New York City, Richmond, Westchester, and Queens) created state churches which authorized salaries for "good and sufficient Protestant ministers."
- North and South Carolina passed similar Establishment Acts in 1706 and 1715.
- Boston officially adopted the Anglican Church in 1685.
- Philadelphia, notwithstanding William Penn, passed a Charter for Christ Church in 1696.

From the time of the Mayflower Compact—
"having undertaken for the glory of God and advancement of the Christian faith,"

through the Plymouth Plantation—
"for the propagation and advance of the gospel of the Kingdom of Christ,"

and on to Virginia's first charter—
"propagating of the Christian religion," the Fundamental Orders of Connecticut ("purity of the Gospel of our Lord Jesus"),

and the New England Confederation—
"advance the cause of the gospel,"

America's founding years were steeped in Christ and Christianity.

America was founded on a basic consensus of Christian principles. John Adams admitted that the American army was "educated in the general Principles of Christianity; and the general Principles, on which the Fathers achieved Independence, were the general Principles of Christianity."

Tolerance of Other Religions in a Christian Nation[9]

Our Founding Fathers openly acknowledged and welcomed the presence of numerous religious groups in America including Buddhists, Muslims, and Jews. John Randolph of Roanoke, Virginia, an early member of Congress, was Muslim. He was later converted to Christianity, discipled by Frances Scott Key, author of the "Star Spangled Banner," and became a strong personal advocate for Christianity.

Dr. Benjamin Rush

Dr. Benjamin Rush, who served in three presidential administrations, was a signer of the Declaration and an evangelical Christian, openly declared:

Such is my veneration for every religion that reveals the attributes of the Deity, or a future state of rewards and punishments, that I would rather see the opinions of Confucius or Muhammad inculcated upon our youth than see them grow up wholly devoid of a system of religious principles. **But the religion I mean to recommend in this place is that of the New Testament**.

The tolerance for other faiths and religions does not negate nor alter the fact that America was founded by Christians on Christian principles. In 1854, following an extensive investigation, the United States Congress declared:

"Had the people, during the Revolution, had a suspicion of any attempt to war against Christianity, that Revolution would have been strangled in its cradle. At the time of the adoption of the Constitution and the amendments, the universal sentiment was that Christianity should be encouraged, but **not any one (denomination) . . . in this age can be no substitute for Christianity . . . That was the religion of the founders of the Republic, and they expected it to remain the religion of their decendants**."

In the U.S. Supreme Court case of *Church of the Holy Trinity v. U.S.* (1892), the U.S. Supreme Court conducted a thorough review of American history.[10] After citing more than sixty historical precedents, the Court concluded:

There is no dissonance in these declarations. There is a universal language pervading them all, have one meaning; they affirm and reaffirm that **this is a religious nation . . . this is a Christian nation.**

John Jay

Some pseudo-historians, not willing to admit truth or historical facts, stand firm in their own personal secularist convictions and proclaim just the opposite, asserting that neither our nation nor its leaders were influenced by Christianity. Some historians go to great lengths in an effort to support the false claim that America was not founded as a Christian nation. They rummage through the nation's historical records in search of facts to support their theory. Unfortunately, there are a great number of Americans today who agree with these characterizations. But let's look further at the facts.

John Jay, our nation's first Chief Justice of the Supreme Court, stated in a letter written in February 1797 to Jedidiah Morse:

"Providence has given to our people the choice of their rulers and it is the duty of, as well as the privilege and interest, of **our Christian nation to select and prefer Christians for their rulers.**"

Jay, one of the three authors of the Federalist Papers, describes America as a Christian nation.[11] Many of the colonial constitutions were explicitly Christian and all affirmed, as do today's state constitutions, a belief in God. The United States Constitution did not nullify the religious views of state constitutions.

Roger Sherman was distinguished as the only Founding Father to sign all four major founding documents: The Articles of Association (1774), the Declaration of Independence (1776), the Articles of Confederation (1777), and the Constitution of the United States (1787). Sherman wrote:

"That a God of infinite Goodness can (through atonement) have mercy on whom He will, consistent with the honor of His law and Government and all of His perfections, is a much better ground of hope than the denial of self-love."[12]

George Washington

George Washington, first President of the United States and an actual participant in the Constitutional Convention, certainly did not separate religion from government. Washington took his oath of office with his hand on an open Bible and swore, "So help me, God" and then bent down and kissed the Bible.[13] It is without a doubt that Washington believed America was a Christian nation. Examples of his written accounts include:

George Washington

- To the Delaware Chiefs on May 12, 1797, Washington said: "You would do well to wish to learn our arts and ways of life, and above all **the religion of Jesus Christ**.... It is the duty of all nations to acknowledge the Providence of Almighty God, to obey His will, to be grateful for His benefits, and humbly to implore His protection and favor."[14]

- In a Proclamation on October 3, 1789, Washington said: "We may then unite in most humbly offering our prayers and supplications to the great **Lord and ruler of nations**, and beseech Him to pardon our national and other transgressions."[15]

- In his first inaugural address, he made reference to "the Almighty Being who rules over the universe; who presides in the councils of the nations; and whose providential aid can supply every human defect." He further said that God's "benediction" is needed to "consecrate to the liberties and happiness of the People of the United States."

- His first Thanksgiving Proclamation (1789) stated, "It is the duty of all nations to acknowledge the providence of Almighty God, to obey His will, to be grateful for his benefits, and humbly to implore His protection and favor." He continued by stating he had been called upon by both houses of Congress "to recommend to the people of the United States a day of public thanksgiving and prayer, to be observed. . . ."

- Washington's Farewell Address (September 19, 1796) stated: "The name of American, which belongs to you, in your natural capacity, must always exalt the just

pride of Patriotism, more than any other appellation derived from local discrimina-
tions. With slight shades of difference, you have the same Religion, Manners, Habits
and Political Principles.... **Of all the dispositions and habits which lead to political
prosperity, Religion and Morality are indispensable supports and in vain would that
man claim the tribute of Patriotism, who should labor to subvert these great Pillars of
human happiness, these firmest props of the duties of Men and Citizens** . . . and let us
with caution indulge the supposition, that Morality can be maintained without
Religion.[16]

Washington's Farewell Address was written with the aid of Madison and Hamilton,
but never orally delivered before the public. Instead it was published in the *Philadelphia
Daily American Advertiser* on September 19, 1796.[17]

Washington said quite clearly, "**Do not let anyone claim to be a true American if they
ever attempt to remove religion from politics.** It is impossible to govern rightly without
God and the Bible."

Washington's statements weren't merely religious in some indefinite sense, but were
expressly Christian. Among his messages to his troops was this from 1776:

"The blessing and protection of Heaven are at all times necessary, but especially so in times of public distress and danger. The general hopes and trusts that every officer and man will endeavor to live and act as becomes a Christian soldier, defending the dearest rights and liberties of his country."

And this from 1778:

"The commander in chief directs that Divine service be performed every Sunday at 11 o'clock, in each brigade which has a Chaplain. While we are duly performing the duty of good soldiers, we certainly ought not to be inattentive to the higher duties of religion. To the distinguished character of a patriot, it should be our highest glory to add the more distinguished character of a Christian."

All of the above looks a lot like religious advocacy in a tax-supported setting (though tax support for Washington's armies was admittedly meager).[18]

The Prayer at Valley Forge copyrighted by Arnold Friberg ©2008 and used by permission from Friberg Fine Art.
For more information visit: www.fribergfineart.com.

Washington lobbied for two years to obtain a chaplain for his command during the French and Indian Wars. After the Declaration of Independence, General Washington, Commander of the Continental Army, ordered regimental commanding officers to obtain chaplains to serve at the Continental Congress. Washington ordered his commanders:

"See that all inferior officers and soldiers pay them [chaplains] a suitable respect and attend carefully upon religious exercises. **The blessing and protection of Heaven are at all times necessary, but especially so in times of public distress and danger**—The General hopes and trusts, that every officer and man, will endeavor so to live, and act as becomes a Christian Soldier defending the dearest Rights and liberties of his country."

"It is impossible to account for the creation of the universe without the agency of A SUPREME BEING. It is impossible to govern the universe without the aid of A SUPREME BEING. It is impossible to reason without arriving at A SUPREME BEING."

—George Washington

On September 25, 1789—the day they adopted the First Amendment—Congress directed a joint committee of both houses to request President Washington to recommend a day of public thanksgiving and prayer to Almighty God for the peaceful manner in which the Constitution had been established.

In addition to the U.S. Constitution signed on the 17th day of September, "in the Year of our Lord 1789," the Constitution continues "and of the Independence of the United States of America the twelfth, in witness whereof we have hereunto subscribed our names," and was signed by President George Washington, referring to the Independence of the United States (which mentions God four times).

General Washington was selected to preside over the Constitutional Convention. He set the tone of the gathering soon after his arrival in Philadelphia.

> "If to please the people we offer what we ourselves disapprove, how can we afterwards defend our work? Let us raise a standard to which the wise and the honest can repair; the event is in the hands of God."
> —*General George Washington, Constitutional Convention, Philadelphia, PA*

Some biographers have attempted to characterize Washington as a deist saying that he had a general belief in God but did not subscribe to Bible-based Christianity. Washington often talked of God as Providence, the Creator, the Supreme Being, and Great Lord and Ruler of Nations, using nonsectarian names. He did not use terms such as "Savior" and "Redeemer." But he did speak in Judeo-Christian traditions such as in his Thanksgiving Proclamation (1789), imploring God for "His protection and favor." If he were a deist, Washington would not ask God to intervene.

Washington did not advocate a separation of faith and public life, thinking that removing religion from the public square would violate freedom of expression. Washington felt that religion was a strong part of American life and that "religion and morality were key to the nation's survival."[19]

Washington was a Christian statesman par excellence. For example, he was unanimously elected twice as President of the United States without opposition. He refused ever to take any salary for that position and set an unbelievable example for future presidents. They tried to make him a king several times, but he always refused the offer. They would have had him continue running for office, but he said that for the good of his country, he would retire after his second term. He set before us a remarkable example of a statesman and of a Christian.[20]

John Adams

Christian Views of Other Early Leaders

JOHN ADAMS

Christian men continued Washington's example. Not too different from Washington's comments were those of his successor, John Adams of Massachusetts. Adams frequently expressed in both private and public statements the belief that political liberty required religious virtue. As he wrote to his wife Abigail in 1775:

"Statesmen may plan and speculate for liberty, but it is Religion and Morality alone which can establish the principles upon which freedom can securely stand. **A patriot must be a religious man**."

Adams would reinforce this view in public statements when he became the country's leader. In his presidential proclamation of 1798, he urged his fellow citizens to "acknowledge before God the manifold sins and transgressions with which we are justly chargeable . . . beseeching Him at the same time of His infinite grace, through the Redeemer of the world, freely to remit all offenses and to incline us by His holy Spirit to . . . repentance and reformation."[21]

He also said:

"The general principles on which the Fathers achieved Independence were ... the general principles of Christianity.... I will avow that I then believed, and now believe, that those general principles of Christianity are as eternal and immutable as the existence and attributes of God; and that those principles of liberty are as unalterable as human nature."

John Quincy Adams

In a letter to the Third Division of the Militia of Massachusetts on October 11, 1798, John Adams wrote, "Our Constitution was made only for a moral and religious people. It is wholly inadequate to the government of any other."[22] He also said, "Let them revere nothing but religion, morality, and liberty."[23]

JOHN QUINCY ADAMS

John Quincy Adams, distinguished statesman, who served as America's sixth president, and as senator, congressman, secretary of state, and foreign minister to France and Great Britain, said Christianity is "indissolubly linked" to the founding of America.[24] On July 4, 1837, he asked,

"Why is it that next to the birthday of the **Savior of the World**, your most joyous and most venerated festival returns on this day? ... Is it not that in the chain of human events, the birthday of the nation is indissolubly linked with the birthday of the Savior? That it forms a leading event in the progress of the Gospel dispensation? Is it not that the

Declaration of Independence first organized the social compact on the foundation of the Redeemer's mission upon earth? That it laid the cornerstone of human government upon the first precepts of Christianity?"

These were strong words that might, if uttered today, provoke a media-fed firestorm of protest but uncontroversial when spoken by this venerable patriot who served our nation so long and so well.

It is no slight testimonial both to the merit and the worth of Christianity, that in all the ages since its promulgation, the great mass of those who have risen to imminence by the profound wisdom and integrity have recognized and reverenced Jesus of Nazareth as the Son of the Living God.

In his inaugural address on March 4, 1825, John Quincy Adams said:

"I shall look for whatever success may attend my public service, and knowing that 'Except the Lord keep the city the Watchman waketh but in vain,' with fervent supplications for His favor, **to His overruling providence I commit with humble but fearless confidence my own fate and the future destinies of my country**.

James Madison

"We have this day restored the Sovereign to Whom all men ought to be obedient. He reigns in heaven and from the rising to the setting of the sun, let His Kingdom come.

"The Declaration of Independence first organized the social compact on the foundation of the Redeemer's mission.... [I]t laid the cornerstone of human government upon the first precepts of Christianity."

During his speech commemorating the Declaration of Independence, July 4, 1837, he said:

"The highest glory of the American was this: it **connected in one indissoluble bond the principles of civil government with the principles of Christianity**. From the day of the Declaration . . . they [the American people] were bound by the laws of God, which they all, and by the laws of the gospel, which they nearly all, acknowledge as the rules of their conduct."

Samuel Adams

JAMES MADISON

James Madison, Jefferson's political ally and successor in the White House, is likewise cited in the standard histories, as he did hold separationist views, up to a point and with provisos. Yet he was not a skeptic, but a believing Christian. He was a protegé of the Calvinist John Witherspoon at Princeton, read theology with his mentor, and maintained his interest in the subject for years thereafter. Between 1772 and 1775 he undertook an extensive study of Scripture at Montpelier. His papers include notes on the Bible made at this period and a pocket booklet on *The Necessary Duty of Family Prayer, with Prayers for Their Use.*[25]

James Madison fought wording forbidding the establishment of any national religion. It was evident in the first amendment's phrase, "Congress shall make no laws," that the amendment meant what it said and said what it meant. The Federal Government should not legislate on religious matters and should leave individuals alone in their pursuit of religious truth.

SAMUEL ADAMS

Samuel Adams of Massachusetts, the wily strategist of independence, was an old-fashioned Puritan who saw in America the makings of a "Christian Sparta" not unlike the city on a hill envisioned by his Bay State forebears. He was a moving spirit at the Continental Congress of 1774 in favor of having chaplains lead the group in prayer, despite denominational disagreements. As he put it, "I am not a bigot. I can hear a prayer by a man of piety and virtue, who is at the same time a friend of his country."

Sam Adams was not only a Puritan, but represented a state with an established, tax-supported church—one that would remain established for the next six decades.[26]

> "Let each citizen remember at the moment he is offering his vote that he is not making a present or a compliment to please an individual—or at least that he ought not so to do; but that he is executing one of the most solemn trusts in human society for which he is accountable to God and his country."[27]

PATRICK HENRY

In 1776, Patrick Henry wrote:

Patrick Henry

"It cannot be emphasized too strongly or too often that **this great nation was founded, not by religionists, but by Christians; not on religions, but on the Gospel of Jesus Christ.** For this very reason, people of other faiths have been afforded asylum, prosperity, and freedom of worship here."

Patrick Henry, the firebrand of the American Revolution, is remembered for his words, "Give me liberty or give me death." However, in current textbooks, the context of these words have been omitted. The following is the speech he gave at the Virginia Convention on March 23, 1775 in which those words are contained.

"The question before the House is one of awful moment to this country. For my own part I consider it as nothing less than a question of freedom or slavery, and in proportion to the magnitude of the subject ought to be the freedom of the debate. It is only in this way that we can hope to arrive at truth and fulfill the great responsibility **which we hold to God and our country**. Should I keep back my opinions at such a time, through fear of giving offense, I should consider myself as guilty of treason toward my country and of an act of disloyalty toward the majesty of heaven, which I revere above all earthly kings.

"There is no longer any room for hope. . . . I repeat it, sir, we must fight! An appeal to arms and **to the God of Hosts** is all that is left us!

"They tell us, sir, that we are weak, unable to cope with so formidable an adversary. But when shall we be stronger? Will it be the next week, or the next year? Will it be when we are totally disarmed, and when a British guard shall be stationed in every house? Shall we gather strength by irresolution and inaction? Shall we acquire the means of effectual resistance by lying supinely on our backs and hugging the delusive phantom of hope, until our enemies shall have bound us hand and foot? Sir, **we are not weak, if we make a proper use of the means which the God of nature hath placed in our power.** Besides, sir, we shall not fight our battles alone. **There is a just God who presides over the destinies of nations and who will raise friends to fight our battles for us.** The battle, sir, is not to the strong alone; it is to the vigilant, the active, the brave. Besides, sir, we have no election. If we were base enough to desire it, it is now too late to retire from the contest. There is no retreat but in submission and slavery! Our chains are forged! Their clanking may be heard on the plains of Boston! The war is inevitable—and let it come! I repeat it, sir, let it come!

"It is in vain, sir, to extenuate the matter. Gentlemen may cry, peace, peace!—but there is no peace. The war is actually begun! The next gale that sweeps from the north will bring to our ears the clash of resounding arms! Our brethren are already in the field! Why stand we here idle? What is it that gentlemen wish? What would they have? Is life so dear, or peace so sweet, as to be purchased at the price of chains and slavery? **Forbid it, Almighty God!** I know not what course others may take, but as for me: Give me liberty, or give me death!"

Henry, the stirring voice of the American Revolution, declared in a speech in the Virginia Convention on March 23, 1775, "I know of no way of judging the future but by the past.[28] The past not only judges the future, but also gives purpose to the future. Can we find hope in our heritage?"[29]

Declaration of Independence

The overwhelming majority of the signers of the Declaration and the Constitution were strong, practicing Christians. A late scholar, N.E. Bradford of the University of Dallas, who studied the religious backgrounds of the signers, found that fifty-two of the fifty-six signers of the Declaration were Trinitarian Christians. Similarly, of the fifty-five signers of the Constitution, fifty to fifty-two were Orthodox Christian, "Twenty-nine were Anglicans, sixteen to eighteen were Calvinists, two were Methodists, two were Lutherans, two were Roman Catholics, one lapsed Quaker and sometimes Anglican, and one was open deist." The open deist was Benjamin Franklin, who attended every type of Christian worship, called for public prayer, and contributed to all denominations. It reads:

"When in the Course of human events, it becomes necessary for one people to dissolve the political bands which have connected them with another, and to assume among the powers of the earth, the separate and equal station to which the laws of Nature and of Nature's God entitle them, a decent respect to the opinions of mankind requires that they should declare the causes which impel them to the separation.

"We hold these truths to be self-evident, that all men are created equal, that they are endowed by their Creator with certain unalienable Rights, that among these are Life, Liberty, and the pursuit of Happiness.... We, therefore, the

Representatives of the United States of America, in General Congress, Assembled, appealing to the Supreme Judge of the world for the rectitude of our intentions (and) with a firm reliance on the Protection of Divine Providence, we mutually pledge to each other our Lives, our Fortunes, and our sacred Honor."[30]

✝

Chapter 3

Thomas Jefferson—
The Man, His Beliefs, and His Influence

According to Jefferson's official acts as Governor of Virginia and as President of the United States, civil government must have a religious basis.[1] As Governor of Virginia, Jefferson readily issued proclamations declaring days of "public and solemn thanksgiving and prayer to Almighty God."[2] Jefferson's Virginia "Bill for Punishing Disturbers of Religious Worship and Sabbath Breakers" was introduced by James Madison in the Virginia Assembly and became law in 1786. The law reads:

> "If any person on Sunday shall himself be found labouring at his own or any other trade or calling, or shall employ his apprentices, servants or slaves in labour, other business, except it be in the ordinary household offices of daily necessity, or other work of necessity or charity, he shall forfeit the sum of ten shillings for each such offence, deeming every apprentice, servant, or slave so employed, and every day he shall be so employed as constitution a distinct offence."[3]

Thomas Jefferson

In his Second Inaugural Address (1805), Jefferson stated:

> "In the matters of religion I have considered that its free exercise is placed by the Constitution independent of the powers of the General Government. I have therefore undertaken on no occasion to prescribe the religious exercises suited to it, but have left them, as the Constitution found them, **under the direction and discipline of the church or state authorities acknowledged by the several religious societies**."[4]

Jefferson has been painted an atheist, infidel, deist, and skeptic. It has been claimed he is the guru of separation between church and state, and leader of the effort to eradicate Christianity from America. He is said to be the creator of the secular elite, our secular educational system, the media, and of liberal judges.[5]

The real truth about Jefferson is:

- He attended a Christian school and was taught by Christian pastors.

- He attended the largest church in America at the time, which met Sundays at the same place Congressmen met on Mondays. (Decades later, worship services continued in the completed building in the Rotunda of the United States Capitol, the most visible public building in America.)

- Jefferson first attended church in the House of Representatives two days after he wrote the Danbury letter suggesting that the First Amendment erected a "wall of separation between church and state." On Sunday, January 3, "contrary to all former practice," he went to his first church service in the House, which he attended "constantly" for the next seven years.

- He served on the vestry of the Anglican Church, the equivalent of being an elder in the Presbyterian Church.

- Even though he attended the Anglican church regularly, he also attended Presbyterian, Methodist, and Baptist churches and was particularly thrilled when all four of those denominations held services together in a courthouse.[6]

Church service in the Capitol Statuary Room

- Jefferson included a prayer in each of his two inaugural addresses.

- Thomas Jefferson had 110 personal friends who were clergymen. He encouraged nine of them to run for public office.

- Jefferson supported the church financially. His financial records attest to that, while President, he financially supported ten different churches. Author Mark Beliles points out that Jefferson gave money to "pastors, churches, Bible societies, and Christian schools and colleges."[7]

- He was a daily Bible scholar. As George Washington read the Bible an hour every morning and evening, with prayer, so Jefferson read the Bible in English, Greek, Latin, and French.

- Jefferson signed bills appropriating money for chaplains in Congress and the armed services and signed the Articles of War, which not only provided for chaplains but also "earnestly recommended to all officers and soldiers, diligently to attend divine services."

- He ordered the Marine Band to play for the services.

- He approved churches in the War Office and the Treasury building, with the latter gaining a reputation for more "religious" services because communion was served there.

Jefferson advocated the tax-supported College of William and Mary maintain "a perpetual mission among the Indian tribes," which included the instruction of "the principles of Christianity." Jefferson's proposed curriculum for the University of Virginia included a provision for a "professor of ethics" who would present "the Proofs of the being of God, the Creator, Preserver, and Supreme Ruler of the Universe, the Author of all the relations of morality, and of the laws and obligations these infer."

As Rector of the University of Virginia, Jefferson offered a resolution on reading materials for the law school that listed the Declaration of Independence and Washington's Farewell Address as two of the "best guides" for understanding the "distinctive principles of [American] government."

College of William and Mary

On December 3, 1803, the U.S. Congress, at the request of President Jefferson, ratified a treaty with the Kaskaskia Indians and voted to give an annual subsidy of $100 for the support of a priest for a seven-year period. The duties of the priest were to perform "the duties of his office, and . . . instruct as many . . . children as possible." President Jefferson signed the treaty, which also included money for the "erection of a church." Members of the Congress understood the worth of imparting Judeo-Christian values among the Indians and the need for advancing biblical values.[8]

Similar treaties were enacted with his endorsement for the Wyandot Indians and other tribes in 1806 and the Cherokee in 1807. Another act in 1787 ordained special lands "for the sole use of Christian Indians" and reserved land for the Moravian Brethren "for civilizing the Indians and promoting Christianity." When this act was renewed, it bore the title, "An Act regulating the grants of land appropriated for Military services and for the Society of the United Brethren for propagating the Gospel among the Heathen." Three times during his administration, Congress extended this act and Jefferson signed it into law. Not once did he even consider vetoing it on the basis that it violated the First Amendment or his own "wall of separation" metaphor.[9]

Even though he may be seen by some historians as a nominal Christian, what Jefferson did is totally antithetical to everything the ACLU and others have told the American people. Author Mark A. Beliles has assembled an impressive list of some of his actions as President.[10]

- Promoted legislative and military chaplains.
- Established a national seal using a biblical symbol.
- Included the word "God" in our national motto.
- Established official days of fasting and prayer at least on the state level.
- Punished Sabbath breakers.
- Punished marriages contrary to biblical law.
- Punished irreverent soldiers.
- Protected the property of churches.
- Required oaths be phrased by the words, "So help me, God," and be sworn on the Bible.
- Granted land to Christian churches to reach the Indians with the Gospel.
- Granted land to Christian schools.
- Allowed government property and facilities to be used for worship.
- Used the Bible and nondenominational religious instruction in the public schools. He was involved in three different school districts, and the plan in each required the Bible to be taught in our public schools.
- Funded salaries for missionaries.
- Funded the construction of church buildings for the Indians.
- Exempted churches from taxation.
- Established professional schools of theology.[11]
- Wrote treaties requiring other nations to guarantee religious freedom including religious speeches and prayers in official ceremonies.
- By 1867, the church at the Capitol Building had become the largest church in Washington, D.C., and the largest Protestant church in America,[12] which Jefferson attended.[13]
- In 1801, Jefferson urged local governments to make land available for "Christian purposes."[14]

- Jefferson signed three separate acts setting aside government lands for the sole use of religious groups so that Moravian Missionaries would be assisted in "promoting Christianity."
- In 1801, Jefferson assured a Christian religious school in the newly purchased Louisiana Territory that it would receive the "patronage of the government," and signed his presidential documents with the appellation, "in the Lord Christ."[15]
- Jefferson's non-presidential actions regarding religious expression showed that he called for a state-wide Day of Prayer when he was Governor of Virginia, praised the use of a county courthouse in Charlottesville for religious services,[16] and approved legislation giving legal sanction to religious observances.[17]

Jefferson founded the University of Virginia, designated space in its Rotunda for chapel services, and indicated he expected students to attend weekly divine services.

Jefferson's original draft of the Danbury letter

Unfortunately, much of the historical record of Thomas Jefferson has been excluded from the public debate and, therefore, a false impression of him and his intent has been constructed. Neither at the state nor federal level does Jefferson demonstrate any proclivity toward the obsessive secularization for which the courts have used him.

On January 1, 1802 Jefferson sent a reply to the Danbury Baptist Church with his now infamous "wall of separation" metaphor. However, two days later, on Sunday, January 3, 1802, Jefferson attended church services in the House of Representatives.

Clearly, Jefferson's understanding of his "wall of separation" did not include him and his religious activity, conducted in a government building with operating expenses paid by government funds.[18]

The most noted reference, however, is the now famous letter written by Thomas

Jefferson in 1802 to a group of Baptist pastors in Danbury, Connecticut. In that letter he wrote:

"Believing with you that religion is a matter which lies solely between Man and his God, that he owes account to none other for faith or his worship, that the legislative powers of government reach actions only, and not opinions, I contemplate with sovereign reverence that act of the whole American people which declared that their legislature should 'make no law respecting an establishment of religion, or prohibiting the free exercise thereof,' **thus building a wall of separation between church and state.**"

Significantly, Jefferson's own actions as President miserably fail every religious test contemporary courts have erected in his name, demonstrating that Jefferson would not sanction those tests. Thomas Jefferson saw no violation of the First Amendment in any of his actions.

Most scholars interpret Jefferson's Danbury letter in its context. They accept Jefferson's view that religion is a personal matter that should not be regulated by the federal government, and that the federal government has no power to change law in the states. They interpret the "wall of separation" in the same way as Roger Williams: as a wall to protect God's garden from the world, to protect the church from the government.

Jefferson wrote "I am a Christian..." to Benjamin Rush

In contrast, some secular scholars lift the Danbury letter out of its historical context. They turn the "wall" metaphor on its head and now use it to protect the government from the church, establishing a freedom from religion not known by the Founders. This results in a concerted effort to rid government of any religious influence. Hence, the opposition to Bible reading in schools, official proclamations promoting religious events, nativity scenes in public displays, the posting of the Ten Commandments in and on public buildings, prayer in public places, etc. These scholars fail to recognize that the Danbury Baptists would never have rejoiced at Jefferson's election if he stood for removal of religious influence on the government.

Jefferson kept his religious views private because he believed that "once one started talking about one's religion openly, the public quickly concluded that it had a right to know everything!"[19]

While Jefferson was no atheist, he was no evangelical Christian either. He would only tolerate a religion that fit his conception of reasonableness. He nearly abandoned any appreciation for Christianity until he read Joseph Priestly's *A History of the Corruptions of Christianity* (1793). Through this work and Priestly's *Socrates and Jesus Compared*, Jefferson no longer rejected Christianity, only what he believed were its "corruptions." He alleged the core of Christianity had been obscured by Jesus' disciples and that the Apostle Paul was the first to conceal Jesus' "genuine precepts." By stripping away the corruptions, he contended the true Christian would rediscover the "genuine precepts of Jesus himself."

While Jefferson's opinions are instructive, they remain opinions. His personal correspondence, even as President, has no legal standing. Jefferson's use of the phrase, "wall of separation of church and state" was "a mere metaphor, too vague to support any theory of the Establishment Clause."[20] Yet this metaphor has been adopted as the standard interpretation of the First Amendment.[21] The doctrine of separation cannot be compared to today's absolutist position. According to Jefferson, "opinions" and what a person believes about God—"faith or worship"—are outside the jurisdiction of the state. The state, however, does have jurisdiction over what a person does. As Jefferson wrote to the Danbury Baptists, "The legislative powers of government reach actions only." Can civil governments appeal to religious precepts in the governance of actions?

> *"To the corruptions of Christianity I am, indeed, opposed; but not to the genuine precepts of Jesus himself. I am a Christian in the only sense in which He wished any one to be; sincerely attached to His doctrines in preference to all others."*
>
> —wrote Thomas Jefferson to Benjamin Rush

Jefferson demonstrated his high regard for the ethics of Jesus while maintaining his anti-supernatural worldview of producing *The Life and Morals of Jesus of Nazareth*, a book which is often published as the so-called "Jefferson Bible." There never was a Jefferson Bible per se. Instead, Jefferson cut the miracles from the Gospels in order to produce a book on ethics—the ethics and morals of Jesus Christ for the purpose of evangelizing and educating American Indians.[22] Jefferson studied the Gospel accounts to extract from them what he believed to be the uncorrupted sublime moral teachings of Jesus without the supernatural "additions."

While Jefferson included Luke's account of the birth of Jesus, he omitted references to angels and heavenly announcements pertaining to the event. In addition, "when Jesus performed a miracle in connection with some teaching, the teaching survived, the miracle did not . . . Jefferson included verses detailing the death of Jesus but not the resurrection. No Easter morning sun rises in Jefferson's Bible." His edition of the Gospels ends: "There laid they Jesus, and rolled a great stone to the door of the sepulcher, and departed."

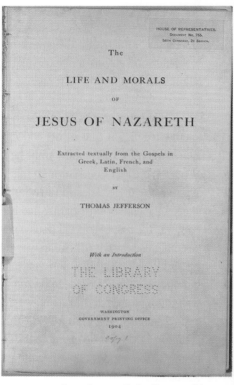

A page from the so-called Jefferson Bible

"The Christian Religion, when divested of the rags in which they (the clergy) have enveloped it, and brought to the original purity and simplicity of its benevolent institutor, is a religion of all others most friendly in the liberty, science, and freest expansion of the human mind."

—Thomas Jefferson

Nevertheless, for all of his anti-biblical statements and beliefs, he understood that "no system of morality would work for the common man or woman 'without the sanction of divine authority stamped upon it.'" Jefferson, the "anti-Christian" and "irreligious infidel," said it is Christ who is our Lord and no one else. Jefferson's famous letter has been greatly perverted and distorted.

"The God who gave us life gave us liberty. And can the liberties of a nation be thought secure when we have removed their only firm bias, a conviction in the minds of the people that these liberties are of the gift of God? That they are not to be violated but with His wrath? Indeed, I tremble for my country when I reflect that God is just; that His justice cannot sleep forever."

—Thomas Jefferson

Some other writings of his include:

"I consider the government of the United States as interdicted from meddling with religious institutions, their doctrines, disciplines, or exercises. This results from the provision that no law shall be made respecting the establishment of religion, or the free exercise thereof, but also from that which reserves to the states the powers not delegated to the United States. Certainly no power over religious discipline has been delegated to the general government. It must thus rest with the states as far as it can be in any human authority." [23]

"God who gave us life gave us liberty. And can the liberties of a nation be thought secure when we have removed their only firm basis, a conviction in the minds of the people that **these liberties are of the Gift of God**? That they are not to be violated but with his wrath? Indeed, I tremble for my country when I reflect that God is just; that His justice cannot sleep forever."[24]

And in a letter to Dr. Benjamin Rush, dated April 21, 1803, he wrote this powerful statement:

"My views ... are the result of a life of inquiry and reflection and **very different from the anti-Christian system imputed to me by those who know nothing of my opinions**."[25]

Virginia Statute for Religious Freedom

The "Virginia Statute for Religious Freedom," written by Jefferson, was in his words, "the severest contest in which I've ever been engaged," wherein Jefferson argued against Patrick Henry, who had his own bill for a tax to support all Christian churches. Henry's bill passed its first two readings in 1784 and seemed certain to pass at the third and final reading.

On January 16, 1786, the Virginia Statute was finally passed, and for Jefferson, it did more than guarantee the freedom to choose a church. It was about intellectual liberty—the freedom of the mind. In "Notes on Virginia," he explained his ideas on government and religious freedom: "The legitimate powers of government extend to such acts only as are injurious to others. But it does mean no injury for my neighbor to say that there are twenty gods or no god. It neither picks my pocket, nor breaks my leg."

The Virginia Statute, acknowledging that "**Almighty God has created the mind free**," and that there should be no departures from the "Holy Author of our religion, who, being Lord both of body and mind ..." and recognizing that "others have established and maintained false religions over the greatest parts of the world ..." that therefore, "no man shall be compelled to frequent or support any religious worship ... or otherwise suffer on account of his religious opinions or belief, but that all men shall be free to profess, and by argument to maintain, their opinions in matters of religion, and that the same shall in no wise diminish, enlarge, or affect their civil capacities."

Jefferson's position, so unlike what has been espoused as truth, was in his own words, one of a Christian. It behooves America today to study the words which communicated his position, and not what some people think he may have said or written.

✠

Chapter 4

The History of Education in America

Dr. Benjamin Rush

"Let the children be carefully instructed to the principles and obligations of the Christian religion. This is the most essential part of education. The great enemy of the salvation of man, in my opinion, never invented a more effectual means of extirpating [removing] Christianity from the world than by persuading mankind that it was improper to read the Bible at schools."
—*Dr. Benjamin Rush, Founder of Public Schools*

America has a long tradition of free schooling for its citizens, and it was the first nation to do so. The first educational establishments were motivated by religious considerations. The Puritans demonstrated their belief in a comprehensive biblical world view in the educational institutions they established. New England was at the forefront of higher education. Harvard College, founded in 1636, was the first to provide a trained ministry just six years after the arrival of the English Christian colonists to the New World.[1]

> ## "The Congress of the United States recommends and approves the Holy Bible for use in all schools."
> —Resolution passed by the U.S. Congress (1782)

Schools and colleges were established for religious purposes. Massachusetts regulated education (1647), and if parents neglected to instruct their children, the local officials could apprentice them so that they could "read and understand the principles of religion and the capitol laws of the country." Connecticut passed a similar law in 1650.

"How is it possible that children can have any just sense of the sacred obligations of morality or religion if, from their earliest Infancy, they learn their Mothers live in habitual infidelity to their fathers, and their fathers in as constant infidelity to their mothers?" —*John Adams, Continental Congress (1776)*

The textbook used by children, *The New England Primer* (1686), mostly contained hymns, prayers, Bible stories, and accounts of Protestant martyrs. It was the first textbook ever printed in America and was used to teach reading and Bible lessons in our schools until the twentieth century. It contained Scripture, the Lord's Prayer, and taught morals and values from a Christian perspective. The Primer is a great example of early American education, introduced in the Boston public schools in 1690. For the next two centuries it was a required textbook from which every first grader learned grammar and spelling.

The 1900 reprint described the impact of the book by stating,

A page from the New England Primer

"The New England Primer was one of the greatest books ever published.... [I]t reflected in a marvelous way the spirit of the age that produced it, and contributed, perhaps more than any other book except the Bible, to the molding of those sturdy generations that gave to America its liberty and its institutions."

The Primer taught first graders the alphabet in several ways. For the letter "A," the young students learned "In Adam's Fall, We sinned all." For the letter "C," the students recited the following: "Christ crucified, For sinners died." Students were later asked, "Who was the first man?" and "Who was the first woman?" Students were also asked, "Who is Jesus Christ?" to which the response is stated, "The Son of God."[2]

Since the Primer was taught in public schools during the 1700s, at the time when the First Amendment was drafted, it is inconceivable that teaching religion in public schools was deemed to be an establishment of religion. The Founders did not believe that religious education in the public schools established an official religion or church.

The U.S. Supreme Court in 1844 stated:

> "Christianity is not to be maliciously and openly reviled and blasphemed against, to the annoyance of believers or the injury of the public . . . such a case is not to be presumed to exist in a Christian country . . . truly, the Christian Religion is a part of the common law of Pennsylvania.
>
> **"Education is useless without the Bible.... The Bible was America's basic textbook in all fields.... God's Word contained in the Bible has furnished all necessary rules to direct our conduct."**

Of the 117 men who signed the Declaration of Independence, the Articles of Confederation, and the Constitution, one out of three had only received a few months of formal schooling and only one in four had attended college. Without exception, they were educated by parents, church schools, tutors, and academies.[3]

Throughout the nineteenth century, almost all of America's publicly funded primary schools provided for readings from the Bible.[4] The Colonists had a Christian philosophy of education—they felt everyone should be educated because each needed to know the truth for themselves. Jefferson, Webster, and Madison all received tutoring from ministers. Even those who attended college were taught by ministers.

The Holy Bible

Schools were church schools started by the major Christian denominations. The first public schools were developed and established in Massachusetts to ensure the children could read and understand the Bible.

*"The Christian religion is, above all
the religions that ever prevailed or existed
in ancient or modern times, the religion of
Wisdom, Virtue, Equity, and Humanity."*
—John Adams

In 1642, the General Court passed legislation requiring each town make sure their children were taught, especially, "… **to read and understand the principles of religion and the capital laws of this country.**"

"Before any man can be considered as a member of Civil Society, he must be considered as a subject of the Governor of the Universe."
—James Madison

In 1647, the "Old Deluder Satan" Act stated, "It being one chief project of that old deluder, Satan, to keep men from the knowledge of the Scriptures…." The General Court ordered any town with fifty families to hire a teacher (who was a minister) so that children might be taught to read and write.

Of the first 108 colleges, 106 were founded on the Christian faith. By the end of 1860, there were almost 246 colleges in America. Seventeen of them were state institutions, many of which were Christian-based. Virtually every other college was founded by Christian denominations or by individuals who declared a religious purpose.

"Religion is the basis and foundation of government."
—James Madison

For example, *Harvard College* was founded in 1636 by Reverend John Harvard who gave half of his property and his entire library to start this Congregational institution. The College's official motto was, "For Christian the Church." The governing rules required both the College's president and professors to "open and explain the Scriptures to his pupils with integrity and faithfulness, according to the best light God shall give him."

Harvard College in Cambridge, MA

The *College of William and Mary* was started as a result of the efforts of Reverend James Blair in order:

"... that the Church of Virginia may be furnished with a seminary of ministers of the Gospel, and that the youth may be piously educated in good letters and manners, and that the Christian religion may be propagated among the Western Indians to the glory of Almighty God."

Yale University was started by Congregational ministers in 170l, "for the liberal and religious education of suitable youth ... to propagate in the wilderness, the blessed reformed Protestant religion."

Princeton, a college closely associated with the first Great Awakening, was founded by the Presbyterians in 1746. Reverend Jonathan Dickson, the first president, declared, "Cursed be all that learning that is contrary to the cross of Christ." Its official motto is: "Under God's Power She Flourishes."

Brown College was started in l764 by the Baptists, and *Rutgers* was started by the Dutch Reformed Church in 1766.

From the very beginning, Christianity was the foundational religion of America, and for centuries, it has been planted in the hearts of Americans through the home and private and public schools. Our continued growth and prosperity depend upon the manner in which we educate the youth of America on the principles of the Christian religion.

Informed, Godly Citizens Needed

The framers of the Constitution spoke eloquently about the fact that only a moral people—a nation of informed, godly citizens with common spiritual and social value—were capable of self-government. They could not have envisioned the depths of depravity, lasciviousness, and vice to which our society has fallen—yet they warned of it.

> *"Our Constitution was made only for a moral and religious people. It is wholly inadequate to the government of any other."* [5]
> —President John Adams, October 11, 1798

Historian Paul Johnson said:
"As we have seen, America had been founded primarily for religious purposes, and the Great Awakening had been the original dynamic of the continental movement for independence. The Americans were overwhelmingly church

going, much more so than the English, whose rule they rejected. There is no question that the Declaration of Independence was, to those who signed it, a religious as well as a secular act."[6]

George Washington set the tone for the early school system when he wrote:

"And let us with caution indulge the supposition that morality can be maintained without religion. Whatever may be conceded to the influence of refined education on minds of peculiar structure, reason and experience both forbid us to expect that national morality can prevail in exclusion of religious principle."

The framers of the Declaration of Independence drew many of their ideas from "The Two Treatises of Government," a book which cites the Bible more than 1,700 times to show the proper operation of civil government.

Read the signers' own words about Christianity, the Bible, and God:[8]

- *Samuel Adams, the father of the American Revolution:* "**The right to freedom being the gift of God Almighty** . . . the rights of the colonists as Christians . . . may best be understood by reading and carefully studying the institutions of The Great Law Giver and the Head of the Christian Church, which are to be found clearly written and promulgated in the New Testament."[9]

- *John Adams, also of Massachusetts, second cousin to Samuel and our nation's second president:* "**The Bible is the best book in the world**. It contains more of my little philosophy than all the libraries I have seen; and such parts of it as I cannot reconcile to my little philosophy, I postpone for future investigation."

- *Thomas Jefferson of Virginia, chief author of the Declaration of Independence:* "**The God who gave us life, gave us liberty** at the same time."[10]

- In a letter to Thomas Jefferson on December 25, 1813, *John Adams wrote:* "I have examined all religions, as well as my narrow sphere, my straightened means, and my busy life would allow; and the result is that **the Bible is the best Book in the world**."[11]

- *Patrick Henry* made it even clearer: "It cannot be emphasized too strongly or too often that **this great nation was founded, not by religionists, but by Christians: not on religions, but on the Gospel of Jesus Christ**."[12]

- The First Amendment was to forbid a national church. In his commentary on the First Amendment's original meaning, *Justice Story wrote*: "The real object of the First Amendment was not to countenance, much less advance Mohammedanism, or Judaism, or infidelity, by prostrating Christianity, but **to exclude all rivalry among Christian sects** [denominations] and to prevent any national ecclesiastical patronage of the national government."[13]

- *President Thomas Jefferson also said:* "No nation has ever yet existed or been governed without religion. Nor can be. **The Christian religion is the best religion that has ever been given to man** and I as chief Magistrate of the nation am bound to give it the sanction of my example."[14]

- *Dr. Benjamin Rush of Pennsylvania:* "I know there is an objection among many people to teaching children doctrines of any kind, because they are liable to be controverted. But let us not be wiser than our Maker. If moral precepts alone could have reformed mankind, the mission of the Son of God into all the world would have been unnecessary. The perfect morality of the Gospel rests upon the doctrine which, though often controverted, has never been refuted: I mean the vicarious life and the death of the Son of God."[15]

- *George Washington* warned that: "reason and experience both forbid us to expect that national morality can prevail in exclusion of religious principles."

Noah Webster—America's Schoolmaster

Noah Webster (1758-1843) is recognized by most Americans because of the dictionary that bears his name. His work impacted the areas of law, politics, government, and education. He is known as "America's Schoolmaster." His masterpiece *Dictionary of the English Language* (1928) contained 12,000 words and 40,000 definitions not found in any previous dictionary.

In relation to government, Webster declared:

"Religion which has introduced civil liberty is the religion of Christ and his Apostles, which enjoins humility, piety, and benevolence; which acknowledges in every person a brother or a sister—and a citizen with equal rights.

Noah Webster

This is genuine Christianity and to this we owe our free constitutions of government."
He also wrote:

The moral principles and precepts contained in the Scripture ought to form the basis of all our civil constitutions and laws. All the miseries and evil men suffer from vice, crime, ambition, injustice, oppression, slavery, and war proceed from their despising or neglecting the precepts contained in the Bible."

Concerning education, Webster said:

The Christian religion is the most important and one of the first things in which all children under a free government ought to be instructed ... no truth is more evident to the minds then that the Christian religion must be the basis of any government intended to secure the right and privileges of a free people."

Resolutions

In 1782, the United States Congress voted a resolution which stated:

"The Congress of the United States recommends and approves the Holy Bible for use in all schools."

William Holmes McGuffey, author of the *McGuffey Reader* (used for over 100 years in our public schools with over 125 million copies sold up to 1963) wrote:

"The Christian religion is the religion of our country. From it are derived our nation, on the character of God, on the great moral Governor of the universe. On its doctrines are founded the peculiarities of our free institutions. From no source has the author drawn more conspicuously than from the sacred Scriptures. From all these extracts from the Bible, I make no apology."

William McGuffey

The Fundamental Orders of Connecticut of 1639 read:

"The Word of God requires that to maintain the peace and union of such people, there should be an orderly and decent Government established according to God."

Written in a letter to the editor of the *Sunday School Times* in Philadelphia, Ulysses S. Grant, 18th President of the United States wrote:

A page from the McGuffey Reader

"I believe in the Holy Scriptures, and whose lives by them will be benefited thereby. Men may differ as to the interpretation, which is human, but the Scriptures are man's best guide … I feel very grateful to the Christian people of the land for their prayers in my behalf. There is no sect or religion, as shown in the Old or New Testament, to which this does not apply."

Today's children may not pray or study the Bible in public schools, but as we have seen, early education in this country was quite different. The Bible was an approved textbook and deemed the best book in the world by many of our prominent early leaders.

✠

Chapter 5

Federal and State Governments

The tradition of opening each day with morning prayers first began with the Continental Congress long before there was a Declaration of Independence, Constitution, or Bill of Rights. This practice has been perfectly legal since the beginning of our government's history. Samuel Adams and Thomas Cushing of the Continental Congress were responsible for opening prayers until July 9, 1776, when Duché was elected Chaplain of Congress and delivered the Morning Prayer, reading the 31st Psalm, and made it a political/religious event.

The first time Congress issued a proclamation for days of fasting, prayer, and thanksgiving was on November 1, 1777. On April 7, 1789, Congress appointed a committee to

Congressional proclamation calling for fasting

devise a method for paying chaplains. Strict separationists try to prove the concept of separation of church and state yet ignore this use of morning prayers and paid chaplains in the Congress that continues to this day. If any of our Founding Fathers had the slightest notion of a concept of total separation of church and state, they would not have paid Congressional Chaplains with tax dollars. It was a clear marriage of church and state. From colonial times to the founding of the Republic and ever since, the practice of legislative prayer has coexisted with the principles of religious freedom.

On September 25, 1789, three days after Congress authorized the appointment of paid chaplains, final agreement was reached on the language of the Bill of Rights. Clearly, the men that wrote the First Amendment did not view paid legislative chaplains and opening prayers as a violation of that Amendment. And the practice of opening sessions with prayer has continued without interruption ever since that early session of Congress.[1]

Secularists claim that because of the Constitutional provision banning any religious test to serve in federal public office, faith was not important to the early settlers. Secularists extract this "no religious test" provision and create the following equation: "No religious test = no public religious expression." This equation misconstrues the nature of the religious "test ban." To the contrary, numerous states had even established churches, and they continued them for many years.[2] These states also contained similar religious "test bans" in their own constitutions.[3] Therefore, whatever the proposed effect of the religious "test ban," the purpose of such bans was not to eliminate public religious expressions.[4]

Article I, Section 2 states: "The House of Representatives shall be composed of Members chosen every second Year by the People of the several States, and the Electors in each State shall have the Qualifications requisite for Electors of the most numerous Branch of the State Legislature."[5] Thus, eligibility for service as a representative in the House pivoted on state-erected requirements.[6] Most states had "religious tests" as conditions for suffrage,[7] and therefore, it could not be the case that these religious tests violated the Constitution.[8] The Constitution itself used those tests when it incorporated the practice of the several states into the election qualifications for congressmen.[9],[10]

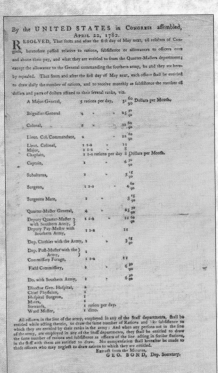

Congress approved chaplain's pay.

The significance of the following provision is that in the cultural atmosphere of the day, Sunday was the day set aside for worship.[11] And again, with Puritan Sunday service as a dominant cultural backdrop for the New World,[12] the Founders did not want to require the President to labor on the Lord's Day.[13]

"Every Bill which shall have passed the House of Representatives and the Senate, shall, before it becomes a Law, be presented to the President of the Untied States; If he approves, he shall sign it, but if not he shall return it, with his Objections to that House in which it shall have originated, who shall enter the Objections at large on their Journal, and proceed to reconsider it.... If any Bill shall not be returned by the President within ten Days (Sundays excepted) after it shall have been presented to him, the Same shall be a Law, in like Manner as if he had signed it, unless the Congress by their Adjournment prevent its Return, in which Case it shall not be a Law."[14]

In 1800, Congress authorized the public use of the Capitol for Christian worship services to occur each Sunday.[15] By 1860, multiple services were occurring.[16] There was no objection that this practice somehow violated the supposed "wall of separation"[17] between church and state.[18] Rather, the Constitution itself is manifestly friendly to the "religious rhythm" of the culture."[19]

State Constitution Preambles

The state constitutions also based their authority on the Christian religion, though perhaps not to the extent that the colonial charters did. State constitutions were filed with religious references permitting varying amounts of religious freedom. Contrary to current understanding, at least eight of the American colonies in 1775 had established churches that were preferred, sanctioned, and supported by the state. Even Supreme Court Justice Hugo Black acknowledged this fact in of all places, his majority opinion banning voluntary public school prayer. Black wrote, "Indeed as late as the time of the Revolutionary War, there were established churches in at least eight of the thirteen former colonies and established religions in at least four of the other five." Other scholars have said that at least nine of the thirteen colonies had established churches at the time.[20]

Justice Hugo Black

To show how much importance each state placed on God, the following are introductory phrases in the Preambles to their state constitutions:

ALABAMA, 1901: "We, the people of the State of Alabama ... invoking the favor and guidance of Almighty God do ordain and establish the following Constitution...."

ALASKA, 1956: "We the people of Alaska, grateful to God and to those who founded our nation and pioneered this great land...."

ARIZONA, 1911: "We the people of the State of Arizona, grateful to Almighty God for our liberties, do ordain this Constitution...."

ARKANSAS, 1874: "We the people of the State of Arkansas, grateful to Almighty God for the privilege of choosing our own form of government...."

CALIFORNIA, 1879: "We, the people of the State of California, grateful to Almighty God for our freedom...."

COLORADO, 1876: "We, the people of Colorado, with profound reverence for the Supreme Ruler of the Universe...."

CONNECTICUT, 1818: "The people of Connecticut, acknowledging with gratitude the good Providence of God in permitting them to enjoy...."

DELAWARE, 1897: "Through Divine Goodness all men have, by nature, the rights of worshipping and serving their Creator according to the dictates of their consciences...."

FLORIDA, 1885: "We, the people of the State of Florida, grateful to Almighty God for our constitutional liberty, establish this constitution...."

GEORGIA, 1777: "We, the people of Georgia, relying upon the protection and guidance of Almighty God, do ordain and establish this constitution...."

HAWAII, 1959: "We, the people of Hawaii, grateful for Divine Guidance ... establish this constitution...."

IDAHO, 1889: "We, the people of the State of Idaho, grateful to Almighty God for our freedom, to secure its blessings...."

ILLINOIS, 1870: "We, the people of the State of Illinois, grateful to Almighty God for the civil, political and religious liberty which He hath so long permitted us to enjoy and looking to Him for a blessing on our endeavors...."

INDIANA, 1851: "We, the People of the State of Indiana, grateful to the Almighty God for the free exercise of the right to close our form of government...."

IOWA, 1856: "We, the People of the State of Iowa, grateful to the Supreme Being for the blessings hitherto enjoyed, and feeling our dependence on Him for a continuation of these blessings, establish this Constitution...."

KANSAS,1859: "We, the people of Kansas, grateful to Almighty God for our civil and religious privileges, establish this Constitution...."

KENTUCKY, 1891: "We, the people of the Commonwealth of Kentucky ... grateful to Almighty God for the civil, political and religious liberties...."

LOUISIANA, 1921: "We, the people of the State of Louisiana, grateful to Almighty God for the civil, political and religious liberties we enjoy...."

MAINE, 1820: "We the People of Maine ... acknowledging with grateful hearts the

Stained glass depicting prayer at the first Congress 1774

goodness of the Sovereign Ruler of the Universe in affording us an opportunity ... and imploring His aid and direction...."

MARYLAND, 1776: "We, the people of the State of Maryland, grateful to Almighty God for our civil and religious liberty...."

MASSACHUSETTS, 1780: "We ... the people of Massachusetts, acknowledging with grateful hearts, the goodness of the Great Legislator of the Universe ... in the course of His Providence, and opportunity ... and devoutly imploring His direction...."

MICHIGAN, 1908: "We, the people of the State of Michigan, grateful to Almighty God for the blessings of freedom, establish this Constitution...."

MINNESOTA, 1857: "We, the people of the State of Minnesota, grateful to God for our civil and religious liberty, and desiring to perpetuate its blessings...."

MISSISSIPPI, 1890: "We, the people of Mississippi, in convention assembled, grateful to Almighty God, and invoking His blessing on our work...."

MISSOURI, 1845: "We, the people of Missouri, with profound reverence for the Supreme Ruler of the Universe, and grateful for His goodness ... establish this Constitution...."

MONTANA, 1889: "We, the people of Montana, grateful to Almighty God for the blessings of liberty, establish this Constitution...."

NEBRASKA, 1875: "We, the people, grateful to Almighty God for our freedom ... establish this Constitution...."

NEVADA, 1864: "We the people of the State of Nevada, grateful to Almighty God for our freedom, establish this Constitution...."

NEW HAMPSHIRE, 1792 – PART I, ART. I, SEC. V: "Every individual has a natural and unalienable right to worship God according to the dictates of his own conscience."

Congressional proclamation calling for Thanksgiving

NEW JERSEY, 1844: "We, the people of the State of New Jersey, grateful to Almighty God for civil and religious liberty which He hath so long permitted us to enjoy, and looking to Him for a blessing on our endeavors...."

NEW MEXICO, 1911: "We, the people of New Mexico, grateful to Almighty God for the blessings of liberty, in order to secure the advantages of a state government, do ordain and establish this Constitution."

NEW YORK, 1846: "We the people of the State of New York, grateful to Almighty God for our freedom, in order to secure its blessing...."

NORTH CAROLINA, 1868: "We the people of the State of North Carolina, grateful to

Almighty God, the Sovereign Ruler of Nations, for our civil, political, and religious liberties, and acknowledging our dependence upon Him for the continuation of those...."

NORTH DAKOTA, 1889: "We, the people of North Dakota, grateful to Almighty God for the blessings of civil and religious liberty, do ordain...."

OHIO, 1852: "We the people of the State of Ohio, grateful to Almighty God for our freedom, to secure its blessings and to promote our common...."

OKLAHOMA, 1907: "Invoking the guidance of Almighty God, in order to secure and perpetuate the blessings of liberty ... establish this...."

OREGON, 1857 – BILL OF RIGHTS, ARTICLE I, SECTION 2: "All men shall be secure in the Natural right, to worship Almighty God according to the dictates of their consciences...."

PENNSYLVANIA, 1776: "We, the people of Pennsylvania, grateful to Almighty God for the blessings of civil and religious liberty, and humbly invoking His guidance...."

RHODE ISLAND, 1842: "We, the people of the State of Rhode Island, grateful to Almighty God for the civil and religious liberty which He hath so long permitted us to enjoy, and looking to Him for a blessing...."

SOUTH CAROLINA, 1778: "We, the people of the State of South Carolina, grateful to God for our liberties, do ordain and establish this constitution...."

SOUTH DAKOTA, 1889: "We, the people of South Dakota, grateful to Almighty God for our civil and religious liberties ... establish this...."

TENNESSEE, 1796 – ARTICLE XI.III: "That all men have a natural and indefeasible right to worship Almighty God according to the dictates of their conscience...."

Draft of the Texas State Constitution

TEXAS, 1845: "We, the People of the Republic of Texas, acknowledging, with gratitude, the grace and beneficence of God...."

UTAH, 1896: "Grateful to Almighty God for life and liberty, we establish this Constitution...."

VERMONT, 1777: "Whereas all government ought to ... enable the individuals who compose it to enjoy their natural rights, and other blessings which the Author of Existence has bestowed on man...."

VIRGINIA, 1776 – BILL OF RIGHTS, XVI: "Religion, or the Duty which we owe our Creator ... can be directed only by Reason ... and that it is the mutual duty of all to practice Christian Forbearance, Love and Charity towards each other...."

WASHINGTON, 1889: "We, the People of the State of Washington, grateful to the Supreme Ruler of the Universe for our liberties, do ordain this Constitution...."

WEST VIRGINIA, 1872: "Since through Divine Providence we enjoy the blessings of civil, political and religious liberty, we the people of West Virginia reaffirm our faith in and constant reliance upon God...."

WISCONSIN, 1848: "We, the people of Wisconsin, grateful to Almighty God for our freedom, domestic tranquility...."

WYOMING, 1890: "We, the people of the State of Wyoming, grateful to God for our civil, political, and religious liberties ... establish this Constitution...."

Washington being sworn into office

✠

Chapter 6

Men Who Helped Shape U.S. Policy

The Federalist Papers

The Federalist Papers are a series of 85 articles, published in 1787-88 advocating the ratification of the United States Constitution. The Federalist Papers serve as a primary source for interpretation of the Constitution, as they outline the philosophy and motivation of the proposed system of government. The authors of the Federalist Papers wanted to both influence the vote in favor of ratification and shape future interpretations of the Constitution. The authors of the Federalist Papers were Alexander Hamilton, James Madison, and John Jay. These men did as much as any others to ensure ratification of the Constitution through their profound and learned defense of its principles.

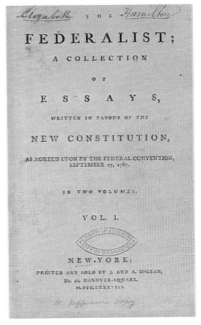

The Federalist Papers

Hamilton said: "I have carefully examined the evidences of the Christian religion, and if I was sitting as a juror upon its authenticity I would unhesitatingly give my verdict in its favor. I can prove its truth as clearly as any proposition ever submitted to the mind of man."

Hamilton helped form the Christian Constitutional Society whose objectives were "the support of the Christian religion" and "the support of the United States." Madison, a committed Christian, "Father of the Constitution," and fourth President of the United States, spoke 161 times at the Constitutional Convention, second only to Governor Morris. Madison studied at Princeton under the nation's foremost theologian, Reverend John Witherspoon. Madison said, "Religion is the basis and foundation of Government." His personal notes in his Bible make clear he firmly believed in the divinity of Jesus Christ.

Benjamin Franklin

Benjamin Franklin drafted a state-wide prayer proclamation for his state of Pennsylvania.[1] Franklin also recommended Christianity in the state's public schools[2] and worked to raise church attendance in his state. He desired to start a colony in Ohio with Reverend George Whitfield to:

Benjamin Franklin

"... facilitate the introduction of pure religion among the heathen [in order to show the Indians] a better sample of Christians than they commonly see in our Indian traders. In such an enterprise, I could spend the remainder of life with pleasure, and **I firmly believe God would bless us with success**."[3]

The following remarks were made by Franklin in a letter to the President of the United States:

Mr. President:

The small progress we have made after four or five weeks of close attendance and continual reasoning with each other, our different sentiments on almost every question, several of the last producing as many noes as ayes, is methinks, a melancholy proof of the imperfection of the Human Understanding....

In the beginning of the contest with Great Britain, when we were sensible of danger, **we had daily prayer in this room for Divine protection.** [The First Congress met in 1774.] Our prayers, Sir, were heard and they were graciously answered. **All of us who were engaged in the struggle must have observed frequent instances of a superintending Providence in our favor.**

To that kind Providence we owe this happy opportunity of consulting in peace on the means of establishing our future national felicity. And have we now forgotten that powerful Friend? Or do we imagine we no longer need His assistance? **I have lived, Sir, a long time, and the longer I live, the more convincing proofs I see of this truth: that God governs in the affairs of men.** And if a sparrow cannot fall to the ground without His notice, is it probable that an empire can rise without His aid?

We have been assured, Sir, in the Sacred Writings, that "Except the Lord build the house, they labor in vain that build it." I firmly believe this; and I also believe that without His concurring aid, we shall succeed in the political building no better than the builders of Babel: We shall be divided by our partial local interests; our projects will be confounded, and we ourselves shall become a reproach and byword down to future ages.

And what is worse, mankind may hereafter, from this unfortunate instance, despair of establishing Governments by Human wisdom and leave it to chance, war, and conquest.

I therefore beg leave to move that henceforth prayers imploring the assistance of Heaven, and its blessing on our deliberations, be held in this Assembly every morning before we proceed to business, and that one or more of the clergy of this city be requested to officiate in that service.

Franklin made one of the nation's most forceful defenses of religion when it was attacked by Thomas Paine, author of the infamous "Age of Reason." Franklin cited numerous Bible verses to prove his point. He also called for the establishment of chaplains and daily prayer at the Constitutional Convention. He did all this, yet Franklin is described as one of the "least religious" of the Founding Fathers!

> "A Bible and a newspaper in every house, a good school
> in every district—all studied and appreciated—as their merit are the
> principle support of virtue, morality and civil liberty."
> —*Benjamin Franklin (March 1778)*

"Here is my creed. **I believe in one God, the Creator of the universe. That he governs it by his providence.** That he ought to be worshiped. That the most acceptable service we render to him is doing good to his other children. That the soul of man is immortal and will be treated with justice in another life respecting its conduct in this."   —*Benjamin Franklin*[4]

Joseph Story[5]

Joseph Story was on the Supreme Court for 34 years, serving with Chief Justice John Marshall, and is considered the founder of the Harvard Law School. Joseph Story was one of the most noted historical commentators on the U.S. Constitution.[6] What he wrote in his 1833 volume, *Commentaries on the U.S. Constitution*, proves that the Founding Fathers had a vastly different view of religion and government from what the ACLU wants

Americans to believe today. In his Familiar Exposition of the Constitution of the United States 1840, Story wrote:

> "Probably at the time of the adoption of the constitution, and of the amendment to it … sentiment in America was that **Christianity ought to receive encouragement from the state**, so far as it is not incompatible with the private rights of conscience, and the freedom of religious worship.[7]

> "In fact, every American colony, from its foundation down to the revolution, with the exception of Rhode Island … did openly, by the whole course of its laws and institutions, support and sustain, in some form, the Christian religion, and almost invariably gave a peculiar sanction to some of its fundamental doctrines…. Indeed, in a republic, there would seem to be a peculiar propriety in viewing the Christian religion, as the great basis on which it must rest for its support and permanence, if it be, what it has been deemed by its truest friends to be, the religion of liberty."[8]

Joseph Story

We are not to attribute this prohibition of a national religious Establishment First Amendment to an indifference to religion in general, and especially to Christianity (which none could hold in more reverence than the framers of the Constitution).

Given that he was appointed to the bench by James Madison, that his Commentaries on the Constitution were the reference of record among early American lawyers, and that he helped to shape the nation's jurisprudence for nearly half a century, Story's understanding of the meaning of the First Amendment should be taken as definitive.[9]

Joseph Story was known as the "Father of American Jurisprudence." The following are some of his forceful statements:

> America is a "Christian country…. Christianity … is not to be maliciously and openly blasphemed against. It is necessary for us … to consider the establishment of a school or college, for the propagation of Deism or any other form of infidelity. Such a case is not presumed to exist in a Christian country." —*Vidal v. Girard's Executors (1844)*

"Probably at the time of the adoption of the Constitution, and of the amendment to it now under consideration [the First Amendment], the general if not the universal sentiment in America was that Christianity ought to receive encouragement from the State so far as was not incompatible with the private rights of conscience and the freedom of religious worship. Any attempt to level all religions, and to make it a matter of state policy to hold all in utter indifference, would have created universal disapprobation, if not universal indignation."[10]

"One of the beautiful boasts of our municipal jurisprudence is that Christianity is a part of the Common Law.... There never has been a period in which the Common Law did not recognize Christianity as lying at its foundations.... I verily believe Christianity necessary to the support of civil society."

"God save the United States and this Honorable Court."
—*Invocation given in the U.S. Supreme Court and all federal courts since the days of Chief Justice John Marshall*

John Locke

Where did our Founders find the ideas that made the Declaration the most successful government document in the history of the world? James Otis, mentor of Samuel Adams and John Hancock said, "The authority of Mr. Locke has . . . been preferred to all others." Declaration signers such as John Adams, Benjamin Franklin, Thomas Jefferson, Benjamin Rush, and many others sang the praises of John Locke.

Benjamin Rush said, "The Declaration of Independence [was] . . . founded upon one and the same theory of government . . . expounded in the writing of Locke."[11]

John Locke had a powerful political influence on America and the Declaration of Independence, but critics today try to classify Locke as a deist. Not only was John Locke considered a theologian by previous generations, but Locke even wrote a verse-by-verse commentary on Paul's Epistles and compiled a topical Bible which he called a "Common-place Book to the Holy Bible" that listed the verses in the Bible, subject by subject.

When antireligious "enlightened" thinkers attacked Christianity, Locke defended his beliefs in his book, *The Reasonableness of Christianity as*

John Locke

Delivered in the Scriptures. Locke wrote a number of other books on Christianity, but the writing of Locke that most influenced the Founders' philosophy in the Declaration of Independence was his *Two Treatises of Government.* A signer of the Declaration, Richard Henry Lee, declared that the Declaration itself was "copies from Locke's Treatise on Government." Even though it is less than 400 pages in length, he refers to the Bible more than 1500 times to show the proper operation of civil government.

John Jay[12]

John Jay was the first Chief Justice of the United States Supreme Court. In October 1816, he said:

"The Bible is the best of all books, for it is the word of God and teaches us the ways to be happy in this world and in the next. Continue therefore to read it and to regulate your life by its precepts. Providence as given to our people the choice of their rulers, and it is the duty, as well as the privilege and interest of our Christian nation, to select and prefer Christians for their rulers."
—*John Jay, co-author of the Federalist Papers, first Chief Justice of the U.S. Supreme Court*

Today, these words would never meet the criteria for being "politically correct," but in those days, the thread that was carefully woven throughout their lives was formed on the principles of Christianity and faith in Jesus Christ.

Daniel Webster

Webster had a political career spanning four decades. Considered one of the greatest orators in American history, he was Secretary of State for three presidents, a U.S. Senator, Congressman, and is esteemed as one of the five greatest senators in U.S. history.[13] Webster said:

"If there is anything in my thoughts or style to command, the credit is due to my parents for instilling in me an early love of the Scriptures. **If we abide in the principles taught in the Bible, our country will go on prospering** and to prosper; If we and our posterity shall be true to the Christian religion, and if we and they shall live always in the fear of God and respect His commandments … we may have the highest hopes of the future fortunes of our country.…

Daniel Webster

"But if we in our posterity neglect religious instruction and authority, violate the rules of eternal justice, trifle with the injunctions of morality, and recklessly destroy the political constitution which holds us together, no man can tell how sudden a catastrophe may overwhelm us and bury all our glory in profound obscurity."[14]

Webster also said:

"The Christian religion—its general principles—must ever be regarded among us as the foundation of civil society."

Sir William Blackstone

Commentaries on the Laws of England (the most famous law books ever written) by Sir William Blackstone have been abandoned in the humanistic jurisprudence (legal and constitutional philosophy) that permeates contemporary anti-Judeo-Christian judicial decisions.[15] Blackstone is virtually absent from American legal education today. What, then, is the significance of Blackstonian thought to today's law?

The answer is simple. Blackstone's Commentaries are one of the most complete, consistent, humanly authored exposition of the Judeo-Christian worldview of law ever written. His immeasurable influence on both English and American law was universally recognized until well into the twentieth century, although the "bashing of Blackstone" in America began after the Civil War.

"No human legislature has power to abridge or destroy ... [the] rights which God and nature have established, and are therefore called natural rights...."[16]

"When the Supreme Being formed the universe and created matter out of nothing, He impressed certain principles upon that matter from which it can never depart without which it would cease to be ... Man considered as a creature must necessarily be subject to the laws of his Creator ... It is necessary that he should in all points conform to his Maker's will ... this will of his Maker is called the law of Nature ... hence it follows that the first and primary end of human laws is to maintain these absolute (God-given) rights to individuals."

Sir William Blackstone

Several foundational principles are expressed in both the Judeo-Christian worldview and Blackstone's Commentaries:

- The doctrines . . . delivered [by an immediate and direct revelation] we call the revealed or divine law, and they are to be found only in the Holy Scriptures.... Upon these two foundations, the law of nature and the law of revelation, depend all human laws; that is to say, no human laws should be suffered to contradict these.[17]
- God is the Creator of the universe, man, the very concept of law, and several universal laws; and His original Creation was *ex nihilo* ("out of nothing").
- God has built into the universe fundamental laws that are fixed, immutable, and must be obeyed.
- Man is a dependent creature who is not to disobey God's fixed laws but is given free will and reason to discover and choose his actions within the limits of God's laws.
- Man's reason is corrupt and cannot, by itself, discover and apply God's law.
- God is not only the Creator, but a Being of infinite power, wisdom, and goodness.
- God created man and His fundamental laws in such a way that man can be happy only when he is obeying God's law.
- Revealed law, natural law, and human law exist in a clear and inseparable relationship to one another.
- The purpose of human law is to "command what is right, prohibiting what is wrong."
- Human law is not to violate God's law, but is to decide what is right and wrong in regard to "things in themselves indifferent" [i.e., actions that are not intrinsically right or wrong but are declared so by human lawmakers].
- At the time of Creation, God gave man dominion over all the earth, but changes in society ultimately necessitated the emergence of individual property ownership.

The principles of Blackstone's Commentaries are the foundation of our laws. They were a primary legal source book for American lawyers during the early days of the Republic. Blackstone believed all law is derived from God—the God of the Bible.

> "The doctrines thus delivered we call the revealed or divine law, and they are to be found only in the Holy Scriptures. Upon these two foundations, the law of nature and law of [biblical] revelation, depend all human laws; that is to say, no human law should be suffered to contradict these."[18]

Drs. Donald S. Lutz and Charles S. Hyneman analyzed the various sources read and cited by our Founding Fathers.

After a ten-year study, examining over 15,000 political writings of the Founding Era (1760-1805), their research revealed that the most frequently cited authorities of the 180 names examined were Montesquieu, Blackstone, Locke, Hume, Plutarch, Beccaria, Cato,

De Lome and Puffendorf. These researchers concluded the founders cited the Bible vastly more often than any other source. Scripture was cited four times more than Montesquieu or Blackstone and twelve times more than Locke. In fact thirty-four percent of the direct source quotations were from the Bible.[19]

Blackstone was a contemporary of the framers of the U.S. Constitution and provided a primary source for the colonists' understanding of the English Common Law tradition. His writings trained nearly every American lawyer until the mid 19th Century. Sadly, his influence and the Christian world view have since been virtually eradicated from American law schools.

Alexis de Tocqueville

Alexis De Tocqueville (1805-1859) was a French statesman, historian and social philosopher. Arriving in New York in May 1831, he began a nine month tour of the country for the purpose of observing the American prison system, the people, and American institutions. His two-part work, published in 1835 and 1840, "Democracy in America" is the most comprehensive and penetrating analysis of the relationship between character and society in America ever written.[20]

De Tocqueville wrote:

"There is no country in the whole world in which the Christian religion retains a greater influence over the souls of men than in America . . . they brought with them into the new world a form of Christianity which I cannot better describe than styling it a Democratic and Republican religion.

"The sects that exist in the United States are innumerable. They all differ in respect to the worship which is due to the Creator; but they all agree in respect to the duties which are due from man to man."

De Tocqueville provides a unique opportunity to see early America through the eyes of an objective "outsider"—the visiting Frenchman's view of the factors responsible for the American character. Just fifty-five years

Alexis de Tocqueville

after the signing of the Declaration of Independence, the United States of America already had astounded the world with its growth in population, economy, freedom, and prosperity. According to de Tocqueville, America, relative to Europe, was "… much superior in civilization, industry, and power."

Every facet of America's political processes and form of government, cultural dynamics and social factors, are discussed in vivid detail. We learn of our nation's political parties and prison systems, our vast geography, freedom of press and trial by jury, slavery, Indians, war and much else, but de Tocqueville notes, "On my arrival in the United States, it was the religious atmosphere which first struck me."

At the end of his extensive visit, de Tocqueville summarized: "[I]n America, religion leads to wisdom; the observance of divine law guides man to freedom.… I seem to see the whole destiny of America encapsulated in the first Puritan to land upon its shores, just as the first man led to the whole human race.…"

He credits God's divine intervention alone for successful emigration to America: "The founding of New England was a novel spectacle, and everything attending it was unusual and original.… [I]t is the germ of a great nation which God has placed on a predestined shore."

America's early settlers came not only to practice Christianity, but to form a civil society based upon biblical principles: "No sooner had they [the Mayflower Pilgrims] landed on the inhospitable shore than the immigrants turned their attention to the constitution of their society [codified in the Mayflower Compact]."

De Tocqueville noted the intentional partnership between Christianity and government as early Americans wrote their laws: "[T]hey had the bizarre idea of using biblical texts.… The overriding concern of these legislators is the preservation of moral order and good practices in their society.…"

He pays tribute to divine wisdom bestowed upon the early settlers: "It was at that very same time that these same principles, unknown or neglected by European nations, were being proclaimed in the deserts of the New World to become the future symbol of a great nation.… Puritanism was not only a religious doctrine: it linked itself in several respects to the most prominent democratic and republican theories."

Thanks to democracy in America, we have a clear image of the original standards we wish to restore:

"In America you see one of the most free and enlightened nations in the world fulfilling all their public religious duties with enthusiasm.… In France I had seen the spirit of religion moving in the opposite direction to that of the spirit of freedom. In America I found them intimately linked together in joint reign over the same land.… Tyranny may be able to do without faith, but freedom cannot. And what would be done with a nation in control of itself, if it is not subject to God?"[21]

Abraham Lincoln

Abraham Lincoln is immortal in the minds and memories of nearly all Americans. The tall, gaunt, Illinois log-splitter and lawyer is etched in the minds of millions. He remains a figure celebrated and revered in American life.

Lincoln is immortal in the true sense—that of having everlasting life which only Jesus Christ can give to a man. He had been a strong believer in God but largely rejected the doctrines of salvation and redemption. He was already bowed by the burdens of war when Lincoln experienced the almost unbearable, heartbreaking experience of the passing of his beloved son, Willy. When he was asked by his minister if he loved Jesus, he replied:

Abraham Lincoln

"When I left Springfield, I asked the people of Springfield to pray for me. I was not a Christian. When I buried my son, I was not a Christian. But when I went to Gettysburg and saw the graves of thousands of our soldiers, **I then and there consecrated myself to Christ.** Yes, I do love Jesus."[22]

After the conversation, Mr. Noah Brooks, a friend of Lincoln and a noted journalist said, "I've had many conversations with Mr. Lincoln, which were more or less of a religious character, and while I never tried to draw anything like a statement of his views from him, yet he freely expressed himself to me as having the hope of blessed immortality through Jesus Christ."

"All the good from the Saviour of the world is communicated through this Book; but for the Book we could not know right from wrong. All the things desirable to man are contained in it."

—Abraham Lincoln

In the last speech he ever gave, just a few days before his death, Lincoln shared his intention to submit a proclamation for a National Day of Thanksgiving to God. His last act consisted of issuing an edict that every U.S. coin would be printed with the words, "In God We Trust." Lincoln was indeed religious, and it is impossible to discuss him apart from religion.[23]

Lincoln continually talked about "God or a guiding Providence" directing the affairs of men, and filled his speeches, letters, and writings with religious language such as: "The Almighty has His own purposes." "You have, under Providence, performed in this great struggle." "The will of God prevails." "This Nation under God." In short, without reference to the supernatural and Providence, Lincoln would be diminished.[24]

Some of President Lincoln's most noted quotations are:

"I believe the **Bible is the best gift God has ever given to man**. All the good from the Savior (Jesus) of the world is communicated to us through this book.

"Intelligence, patriotism, Christianity, and a firm reliance on Him who has never yet forsaken this favored land, are still competent to adjust in the best way all our present difficulty." *(March 4, 1961, First Inaugural Address)*

Abraham Lincoln, more than any other president in history, used civil religion in his presidency. During the days of the Civil War, he did not emphasize the ways in which God might be on the side of the Union but rather placed God above the nation, standing in judgment for national sins:

"I am not at all concerned … for I know that the Lord is always on the side of the right. But it is my constant anxiety and prayer that I and the nation should be on the Lord's side."[25]

"Both [Northerner and Southerner] read the same Bible and pray to the same God, and each invokes His aid against the other … the prayers of both could not be answered; that of neither has been answered fully. The Almighty has His own purposes." *(March 1865, Second Inaugural Address)*

"… God has destroyed nations from the map of history for their sins. Nevertheless, my hopes prevail generally above my fears for our Republic. The times are dark, the spirits of ruin are abroad in all of their power, and the mercy of God alone can save us.

"It is the duty of nations as well as men to owe their dependence upon the overruling power of God, that you will recognize the sublime truth announced in the Holy Scriptures and proven by all history that these nations are only blessed whose God is the Lord." *(March 30, 1863, Proclamation of a National Day of Humiliation, Fasting, and Prayer)*

"It is meet and right to recognize and confess the presence of the almighty father and the power of his hand equally in these triumphs and in these sorrows … I invite the people of the United States to assemble on that occasion in their customary places of worship and in the forms approved by their own consciences render the homage due to the divine majesty for the wonderful things he has done in the nation's behalf and invoke the influence of his Holy Spirit to subdue the anger which has produced and so long sustained a needless and cruel rebellion." *(July 15, 1863, Proclamation of a National Day of Thanksgiving, Praise, and Prayer)*

Did You Know?

At least 52 of the 56 signers of the Declaration of Independence were orthodox, deeply committed Christians. The other three signers believed in the Bible as the divine truth, in the God of Scripture, and in His personal intervention.

John Quincy Adams

Congress formed the American Bible Society. Immediately after creating the Declaration of Independence, the Continental Congress voted to purchase and import 20,000 copies of the Bible.

Thomas Jefferson, Chairman of the American Bible Society, wrote in the front of his well-worn Bible: "I am a real Christian, that is to say, a disciple of the doctrines of Jesus. I have little doubt that our whole country will soon be rallied to the unity of our Creator."

On July 4, 1821, President Adams said, "The highest glory of the American Revolution was this: It connected in one indissoluble bond the principles of civil government with the principles of Christianity."

"Suppose a nation in some distant region should take the Bible for their only law book, and every member should regulate his conduct by the conscience, to temperance, frugality, and industry; to justice, kindness, and charity towards his fellow men; and to piety, love and reverence toward Almighty God…. What a Eutopia, what a Paradise would this region be." —*John Quincy Adams*

"From the day of the Declaration … they [the American people] were bound by the laws of God, which they all, and by the laws of the Gospel, which they nearly all, acknowledge as the rules of their conduct."
—*John Quincy Adams, July 4, 1835*

President Calvin Coolidge wrote: "The foundations of our society and our government rest so much on the teachings of the Bible that it would be difficult to support them if faith in these teachings would cease to be practically universal in our country."

James Madison

Significantly most other Founding Fathers and early political leaders (whose writings can be located and researched) declared America was guided by and founded on Christian principles. Those founders include Elias Boudinot[26] (President of Congress during the Revolution), Declaration signers Charles Carroll,[27] John Hancock,[28] Benjamin Rush,[29] Stephen Hopkins,[30] as well as Samuel Adams,[31] George Washington,[32] Alexander Hamilton,[33] Rufus King,[34] John Dickinson,[35] Roger Sherman,[36] and Samuel Chase.[37]

James Madison, 4th President of the United States and known as "The Father of our Constitution," stated: "We have staked the whole of all our political institutions upon the capacity of mankind for self-government, upon the capacity of each and all of us to govern ourselves, to control ourselves, to sustain ourselves, according to the Ten Commandments of God."

Part One has only been a snapshot of American history and its early leaders. It discussed the beliefs of our Founding Fathers about God—and more specifically—Jesus and the Christian faith. With these founding beliefs, how did we change our course?

The proof of American Christian history is there for all to read. Our nation's unique experience in freedom is a direct outgrowth of the Christian religion. But, what about the present?

"There is no currency in this world that passes as such a premium anywhere as good Christian character. The time has gone by when the young man or the young woman in the United States has to apologize for being a follower of Christ. No cause but one could have brought together so many people and that is the cause of our Master."
—*William McKinley (1804-1901)*
25th President of the United States

"The Bible ... is the one supreme source of revelation of the meaning of life, the nature of God and spiritual nature and needs of men. It is the only guide of life which really leads the spirit in the way of peace and salvation. America was born a Christian nation. America was born to exemplify that devotion to the elements of righteousness which are derived from the revelations of Holy Scripture."
—*Woodrow Wilson (1856-1924)*
28th President of the United States

"This is a Christian nation. If we ignore the spiritual foundations of our birth as a nation, we do so at our peril. It took a faith in God to win our freedom."
—*Harry S Truman (1884-1972)*
33rd President of the United States

Part Two
THE
PRESENT

Chapter Seven

American Culture Today

As we have so graphically seen in Part One, America became the greatest nation in the world because it was established by a group of faith-filled men and women who intentionally established a nation built upon the principles of the Bible. Their hope was to build a nation that honored God rather than a king.

Where did we go wrong? What cut so deeply into our national fabric? It began with a lie about our nation's roots—the arrogant assumption that America is great because America is smart.

Any mention of God or Jesus Christ is gradually being edited out of classroom history books. Many in America today seek to eliminate any and all references to our religious heritage, even though historical evidences of both our Judeo-Christian heritage and the use of the Bible as a basis for American law abound.

Myths taught as dogma

Imagine trying to teach our children in public schools that God is an intrinsic part of American history as was done in earlier years. Today the liberal education establishment does not want children to know the "absolute laws" found in Scripture (as referred to in the Rhode Island Charter of 1683, which defined the worship of God as a core value). These absolute laws became the basis for our Declaration of Independence.

Many universities in America were founded for the purpose of training ministers. Today, the idea of training men for the ministry would give fits to those who run Harvard University, although it was originally founded to do that very thing. In 1646, Harvard's "Rules and Precepts" required, "Every one shall so exercise himself in reading the Scriptures twice a day that they be ready to give an account of their proficiency therein."

The signs of our Judeo-Christian national heritage are etched in concrete—at least for now. Next time you travel to Washington D.C., visit the Prayer Room in the Capitol building. It features a stained glass window of George Washington praying. When you go to the Washington Monument, Jefferson Memorial, the Tomb of the Unknown Soldier, and the Lincoln Memorial, you'll see inscriptions on these monuments that are replete with references to God and Scripture.

Just a few short decades after the founding of America, Daniel Webster, statesman and America's foremost advocate of nationalism during his day, refused to lose sight of our moral bearings. He said:

> "Our ancestors established their system of government on morality and religious sentiment. Moral habits, they believed, cannot safely be trusted on any other foundation than religious principle, nor any government be secure which is not supported by moral habits."[1]

But today, the simplest of historical traditions is being challenged.

Stained glass of Washington praying

Thanksgiving

Each Thanksgiving, Americans have an opportunity to consider God's grace and blessings to us in Jesus Christ, and reflect upon the words of our Founding Fathers.

President Washington (1789) proclaimed a day of Thanksgiving for "the many signal favors of Almighty God, especially by affording them an opportunity peaceably to establish a Constitution of government for their safety and happiness."

President Lincoln (1863) proclaimed unequivocal gratitude for blessings "which are so constantly enjoyed that we were prone to forget the source from which they come … which are of so extraordinary a nature, that they cannot fail to penetrate and soften even the heart which is habitually insensible to the ever-watchful providence of Almighty God."

We are heirs to the Pilgrims' great legacy. Even if we fail to express our gratitude to the Almighty throughout the year, we should at least give thanks to God on Thanksgiving

Day. It is God and God alone who has given us our heritage and provided us with tremendous blessings.[2]

"Thanksgiving began as a holy day, created by a community of God-fearing Puritans sincere in their desire to set aside one day each year especially to thank the Lord for his many blessings. The day they chose, coming after the harvest at a time of year when farm work was light, fit the natural rhythm of rural life."[3]

The Pilgrims' Thanksgiving was more than a yearning for an autumn celebration with overtones of an English Christmas; it was the Pilgrims' response to God's instruction, "In everything give thanks" (I Thess. 5:18).[4]

Edward Winslow, in his *Chronicle of the History of the Plymouth Colony*, reported the colony's Thanksgiving celebration in which they feasted. He declared, "By the goodness of God, we are so far from want, that we often wish you partakers of our plenty."[5]

the ascriptions justly due to Him for such singular deliverances and blessings, they do also, with humble penitence for our national perverseness and disobedience, commend to His tender care all those who have become widows, orphans, mourners or sufferers in the lamentable civil strife in which we are unavoidably engaged, and fervently implore the interposition of the Almighty Hand to heal the wounds of the nation and to restore it as soon as may be consistent with the Divine purposes to the full enjoyment of peace, harmony, tranquillity and Union.

In testimony whereof, I have hereunto set my hand and caused the Seal of the United States to be affixed.

Done at the City of Washington, this Third day of October, in the year of our Lord one thousand eight hundred and sixty-three, and of the Independence of the United States the Eighty-eighth.

Abraham Lincoln

By the President:

William H. Seward.
Secretary of State.

Lincoln's October 3, 1863 Thanksgiving Proclamation

There are countless official Thanksgiving proclamations. One was passed by Congress on November 1, 1777: "... that it may please God, through the merits of Jesus Christ, mercifully to forgive [our sins] and blot them out of remembrance."

On October 3, 1863, Abraham Lincoln declared a nationwide celebration of Thanksgiving because of "the gracious gifts of the most high God.... To observe the last Thursday in November next as a day of Thanksgiving and praise to our beneficient father who dwelleth in Heaven."

How did Thanksgiving become a grossly secular holiday marked by too much eating, drinking, and football watching, and too little thanksgiving to Almighty God? One reason is that in recent years our children have not been taught about the spiritual aspect of Thanksgiving.

Many elementary school social studies books contain material on the Pilgrims but nothing on the spiritual side of their lives. Professor Paul C. Vitz, who made a comprehensive study of 60 social studies textbooks, wrote, "One social studies book has 30 pages on the Pilgrims, including the first Thanksgiving. But there is not one word (or image) that referred to religion as even a part of the Pilgrims' lives."[6]

The secularization of Thanksgiving has been part of the secularization of America, and both have been going on for a long time.[7] America's Christian history has not been properly taught for many years, and in the process, the origins and meaning of Thanksgiving have been obscured.

Christmas

The political agenda in the war on Christmas has remained largely hidden, a decidedly covert operation. Politics, not religion, is the driving force behind the attempt to put Christmas behind closed doors.

Politically correct folks want to diminish religious influence in America as quickly as possible so that their agenda can become a reality. Using the diversity ruse, they have attacked Christmas as being hurtful and divisive.

Those who are alarmed by the extent of religious belief still prevalent in this country

have roused themselves to call for a *total* separation between church and state. They insist we describe our December holiday as having nothing to do with the birth of Jesus and fight to keep Nativity scenes away from any governmental property. By arguing that our freedoms will be compromised by any reference to Christianity, they have only succeeded in intensifying religious beliefs among the great majority of our people angered by these assaults. That embrace will be strengthened, not weakened, by silly attacks on religiosity.

No court has ever ruled that the Constitution requires government officials to censor Christmas carols, eliminate all references to Christmas, or silence those who celebrate Christ's birth.

Christmas has historically been one of the most celebrated holidays of the American people. In recent years, misconceptions and controversy have led many public officials to remove Christmas from schools, parks, libraries, and government offices. Many school boards have even voted to remove any mention of Christmas from their official school calendars. However, Christians can successfully fight to reinstate Christmas on their local school calendar!

Displaying the Ten Commandments

Every system of government exists to produce and enforce certain laws. Every law necessarily entails a set of moral assumptions. In the deepest sense, the question of every legal system is not whether it will be

Ten Commandments on the Supreme Court

based on religion, but rather which religion or religious philosophy will be its foundation.

Our nation's laws were based on the Ten Commandments. Former President Harry S Truman voiced the prevailing sentiment:

> **"The fundamental basis of this nation's laws was given to Moses on the Mount. The fundamental basis of our Bill of Rights comes from the teachings that we get from Exodus and St. Matthew, from Isaiah and St. Paul.** I don't think we comprehend that enough these days. If we don't have the proper fundamental moral background, we will finally wind up with a totalitarian government which does not believe in rights for anybody."

How times and laws have changed! Although an estimated 4,000 Ten Commandments monuments are displayed throughout the United States, many monuments are coming down because they were challenged by ACLU lawsuits. The ACLU, People for the American Way, and Americans United for Separation of Church and State are strict separationist groups which maintain that the posting of the Ten Commandments is illegal.

However, in Washington, D.C. itself, visitors who enter the National Archives to view the Constitution, Declaration of Independence, and other documents must first pass by a copy of the Ten Commandments prominently displayed in the entryway to the Archives. The U.S. Supreme Court Building has four displays of the Ten Commandments.

Chief Justice Roy S. Moore

Beyond any reasonable doubt, the historical record demonstrates that the Ten Commandments either directly and indirectly have influenced America's founders, leaders, system of government, and legal code. The Ten Commandments are included in a list of publicly acknowledged historical documents which have impacted the founding of America.

John Locke, Hugo Grotius, Sir William Blackstone, Montesquieu, Edmund Burke, George Washington, Benjamin Franklin, James Madison, Noah Webster, Jedediah Morse, Samuel Adams, John Quincy Adams, James McHenry, Alexis de Tocqueville, Daniel Webster, Robert Winthrop, Woodrow Wilson, and hundreds of other public officials, writers, and thinkers have all written of the Ten Commandments being a central part of our philosophy of law and government. But the enemies of our religious freedom are relentless in their efforts to redefine the American way of life. The case of *Glassroth v. Moore* is but one example of their aggression and intolerance.[8]

In 2001, Roy S. Moore, Chief Justice of the Alabama Supreme Court, installed a granite monument in the rotunda of the Alabama Judicial Building to affirm the roots of

American life, liberty, and the law. The monument displayed the Pledge of Allegiance, the National Anthem, the National Motto, and the Oath of all Public Officials, as well as the Ten Commandments.

Stephen Glassroth, an ACLU operative, mounted the charge to remove the display of the Ten Commandments. Glassroth said, "It offends me going to work every day and coming face to face with that symbol."[9] Three "un-civil" liberties groups—the ACLU, Southern Poverty Law Center, and Americans United for Separation of Church and State—hastened to join Glassroth in his effort to stifle the display of the "Big Ten."

Moore said the Ten Commandments document is a depiction of the "moral foundation of the law" and that it would serve to remind all who see it "that in order to establish justice, we must invoke the favor and guidance of Almighty God." Moore believed the

The Ten Commandments monument

question is, "Whether the government can acknowledge God." This is not the same thing as establishing a religion. To ignore the Commandments' role in the shaping of American law requires significant historical revisionism.

But the Ten Commandments granite monument was removed to a storage room, Moore was impeached from office, and the ACLU profited by hundreds of thousands of dollars. *The court ruled that allowing the granite monument inside the building "established" a church in violation of the First Amendment.*

At the close of the hearing before the nine-member body of Judges, Alabama Attorney General William Pryor questioned Moore:

Pryor asked, "Your understanding here is that the federal court ordered that you could not acknowledge God. Is that correct?"

Moore answered, "Yes."

"And if you resume your duties as Chief Justice after this proceeding, you will continue to acknowledge God as you have testified today you would, no matter what any official would say?"

Moore replied: "Absolutely: Without an acknowledgment of God I cannot do my duties. I must acknowledge God. It says so in the Constitution of Alabama. It says so in the First Amendment of the United States Constitution. It says so in everything I have read."

The issue in Alabama was not about the Ten Commandments or a monument. The issue was not about religion. The issue was whether or not the state can acknowledge God.

The Ten Commandments are undeniably a sacred text in the Jewish and Christian faith, and no legislative recitation of a supposed secular purpose can blind us to that fact.... If the posted copies of the Ten Commandments are to have any effect at all, it will be to induce the school children to read, meditate upon, perhaps to venerate and obey, the Commandments. However desirable this might be as a matter of private devotion, it is not a permissible state objective under the Establishment Clause.
—*Stone v. Graham*, U.S. Supreme Court, 1980[10]

Our nation's currency declares our faith.

Encouraging students to obey the Ten Commandments is now illegal. Subsequent U.S. Supreme Court decisions strike down the Commandments if there is any proof they were posted for religious or moral reasons.

If the federal courts are to be consistent in their rulings, they must remove the words "In God We Trust" from the House and Senate Chambers as well as from our nation's currency; the inscription from Leviticus 25:10 from the Liberty Bell; the words from Micah 6:8 found on the walls of the Library of Congress; the psalmist's words that adorn the lawmaker's library; the plaque in the Dirksen Office Building with the words "In God We Trust"; the words of the Jefferson Memorial that read, "God who gave us life gave us liberty"; the words, "Creator, God, and Providence" from the Declaration of Independence; the words, "In the year of our Lord" from the United States Constitution; the phrases, "Almighty God," "piety toward God," "faith in God," "Christian heart," to "spread civilization and Christianity," and "Dedicate this nation before God," that appear on the bronze entablature at Mount Rushmore;[11] and other specific religious/Christian declarations found on government buildings in our nation's capital.[12] To remove these references would reveal clearly that the critics of the Christian foundation of America are trying to destroy our heritage.

Some people seem to have an agenda to erase God and biblical morality from our nation. They perceive any system of moral absolutes that restrains their choices to be antiquated and oppressive. Simply put, the Ten Commandments represent absolute truth, and that cramps their style.

"The First Amendment has been twisted to remove God from public life. Our government officials need to know that there is a God and we can't divorce

ourselves from him. We're moving from separation of church and state to separation of the people from God. If that trend is not stopped, we'll have no rights given by God, only rights given by the government. And what it has given, it can take away."13 —*Judge Roy Moore, Former Chief Justice, Alabama Supreme Court*

Inscriptions on Our Nation's Monuments
Tomb of the Unknown Soldier
Carved on the Tomb of the Unknown Soldier in Arlington National Cemetery is the inscription: Here rests in honored glory an American soldier known but to God.

Tomb of the Unknown Soldier

Washington D.C. Union Station
On the front façade of Union Station, three Scripture verses are engraved: "Thou hast put all things under his feet," "The truth shall make you free," and "The desert shall rejoice and blossom like the rose."

The Lincoln Memorial
The words engraved upon the walls of the Lincoln Memorial reflect the Christian faith and providential perspective of our 16th President. On the south wall is the Gettysburg Address, which ends exclaiming "that this nation, under God, shall have a new birth of freedom—and that government of the people, by the people, shall not perish from the earth."

The Library of Congress
Within the Great Hall of the Jefferson Building are two climate controlled cases: one contains a Gutenberg Bible and the other a hand-copied Giant Bible of Mainz. The display of these two Bibles is appropriate because, in the words of President Andrew Jackson, "The Bible is the rock upon which our republic rests." Many biblical inscriptions can be found on the ceiling and walls including, "The light shineth in darkness, and the darkness comprehendeth it not."

In the Main Reading Room are statues and quotes representing fields of knowledge.

The Lincoln Memorial

Moses and Paul represent religion with the inscription: "What doth the Lord require of thee, but to do justly, and to love mercy and to walk humbly with God." Science is represented by: "The heavens declare the glory of God; and the firmament showeth His handiwork." History is represented by: "One God, one law, one element, and one far-off divine event, to which the whole creation moves."

The Washington Monument

From the tallest structure in Washington, a message of *Laus Deo*—"Praise be to God"—is engraved upon the aluminum capstone on the top of the monument. Inside the structure are carved tribute blocks with many godly messages such as, "Holiness to the Lord," "Search the Scriptures," and "The memory of the just is blessed."

On the 12th landing of the staircase is a prayer offered by the City of Baltimore; on the 20th is a memorial presented by a group of Chinese Christians; on the 24th a presentation made by Sunday School children from New York and Philadelphia quoting Proverbs 10:7—"The memory of the righteous will be a blessing, but the name of the wicked will rot"; Luke 18:16—"Let the little children come to me, and hinder them not for the kingdom of God belongs to such as these"; and Proverbs 22:6—"Train a child in the way he should go, and when he is old he will not turn from it."

President John F. Kennedy's Memorial and Tomb

One of the most famous gravesites in Arlington National Cemetery, marked by an eternal flame, is that of President John F. Kennedy's memorial and tomb. Inscribed upon it is his famous 1961 inaugural address, in which he declared, "Ask not what your country can do for you; ask what you can do for your country." Kennedy's Inaugural Address concluded: "With a good conscience our only sure reward, with history the final judge of our deeds, let us go forth to lead the land we love, **asking His blessing and His help but knowing that here on earth, God's work must truly be our own.**"

John F. Kennedy Memorial

The Washington Monument

The White House

The Capitol Rotunda
All of the eight large paintings in the Rotunda present aspects of our Christian history. It includes art such as: "The Baptism of Pocahontas" and the "Departure of the Pilgrims from Holland," which depicts the Pilgrims observing a day of prayer and fasting.

The White House
An inscription by John Adams, the first president to inhabit the White House, is cut into the marble facing of the State Dining Room fireplace. It reads: "I pray Heaven to Bestow the Best of Blessings on this house and on All that shall hereafter Inhabit it. May none but Honest and Wise Men ever rule under this Roof."

America's Seal
On July 4, 1776, the Continental Congress asked Franklin, Jefferson, and Adams to propose an official Seal. Franklin's vision was biblical, as was Jefferson's. Franklin wanted an image of "Moses standing on the shore, and extending his hand over the sea, thereby causing the same to overwhelm Pharaoh who is sitting in an open Chariot, a crown on

his Head and a Sword in his Hand. Rays from the Pillar of Fire in the clouds leading to Moses, to express that he acts by Command of the Deity. Motto, 'Rebellion to Tyrants is Obedience to God.'" According to historian Derek H. Davis, Jefferson's design included a depiction of "The Children of Israel in the wilderness, led by a cloud by day and a pillar of fire by night."

The front of the Great Seal

The final Seal would not take shape for six years, and the ultimate emblem was simpler—the now familiar eagle. Franklin, Jefferson, and Adams suggested *E Pluribus Unum*—"Out of many, one"—words underscoring the pluralistic nature of the American experiment to be the first of the country's three mottos. However, the mention of God did not disappear entirely. The reverse side of the final Seal (it is the image to the left on the back of the dollar bill) depicts the "Eye of Providence" above an unfinished pyramid with the words of the second motto: *Annuit Coeptis*—**"God (or Providence) has favored our undertakings."** There is also a third Latin motto: *Novus Ordo Seclorum*—"a new order of the ages."[14]

The pyramid signifies strength and duration, and the motto alludes to the many interventions of Providence in favor of the American cause. The date underneath is that of the Declaration of Independence and the words under it, *Novus Ordo Seclorum*, signify the beginning of the new American era in 1776.

The reverse of the Great Seal

Despite the political correctness so prevalent in the media today, American culture, at least at this point in time, still predominantly displays its Christian roots and philosophy. Christians need to take the time to ensure that it continues.

Chapter 8

American Lifestyles

Abortion and homosexuality—two hotly contested political issues—are two actions that people take. They are forms of behavior that have nothing to do with race or gender. Colin Powell writes about the inappropriate linking of homosexual behavior with the Civil Rights movement:

> Skin color is a benign, non-behavioral characteristic. Sexual orientation is perhaps the most profound of human behavioral characteristics. Comparison of the two is a convenient but invalid argument.

Wooden crosses lined up and placed in front of a church to represent aborted fetuses are displayed each January as part of the National Right to Life march.

The state has legitimate jurisdiction in the issues of abortion and homosexuality. Some say that government officials may not intrude into the domain of the bedroom. But abortions do not take place in bedrooms—they are performed in medical facilities regulated by the government.

Liberals only use the bedroom privacy argument as long as it fits their agenda. Homosexuals want laws written to force employers to hire them based on what they do in the bedroom. They want to use the power of the state to teach sexually deviant behavior in schools and force the public to accept what they do sexually.

Homosexuality is chosen behavior.

Carrying this logic through, are we to assume that if child abuse, incest, and assault occur in the sanctity of the home that the State has no jurisdiction to act? Moral anarchists say that consensual acts should not be outlawed.

Homosexuals have always accounted for the vast majority of new HIV-AIDS infections and cost billions of dollars annually. These infections result in much pain and suffering and are accompanied by a high loss of life. This infection mainly occurs as a result of what is done in the bedroom.

Sodomy was a criminal offense in common law and forbidden by the laws of the original thirteen states when they ratified the Bill of Rights. By 1868, when the Fourteenth Amendment was ratified, 37 states had criminal sodomy laws, and until 1961 all 50 states outlawed sodomy. Today, sodomy has been legalized by the U.S. Supreme Court. Justice Antonin Scalia, dissenting in *Lawrence v. Texas* (2003), a U.S. Supreme Court ruling legitimizing sodomy, wrote:

"When the court votes to invalidate the laws of thirty states in order to extend an individual right that cannot be found in the text of the Constitution or traditions of the nation (sodomy), Americans are not alone in their exasperation and anger. These are the same feelings shared by millions of Americans who wonder what guides the Supreme Court at times, other than the personal view of the majority of its justices."

And Judge Robert Bork wrote:
"There is a widespread feeling in America that something is very wrong in our

culture—standards are in a decline.... Popular culture is a disaster; it legit-imized decadent values.... Indeed it is hard to say that there are any standards left that can be enforced by the community, either through law or through social disapproval."

Marriage Under Fire in America

Marriage between one man and one woman is the most ancient, universal institu-tion on earth—the building block of society—and a crucial source of moral order. Marriage was designed to be a fountain for human happiness, but it is at risk of destruc-tion.[1]

Lawyers and politicians made it easier to get a divorce in the 1970s with the no-fault divorce, and predictably, the divorce rate skyrocketed. There was never a law passed that brought so much unhappiness to so many people as the no-fault divorce. Happiness was promised, but misery followed. Studies of couples at the point of getting a divorce have found that five years later, just 22 percent of those who divorced were happy. In contrast, 80 percent of those who decided to stick it out said that five years later they were happy once again.

God's way is the right way! But this is something we often discover too late.

Then the feminist assaulted marriage. Advocates of women's liberation decreed that marriage is a prison for women. Betty Friedman, author of *The Feminine Mystique,* told women that being a housewife is the same as "committing a kind of suicide."

Marriage is not discrimination. Western Civilization would not be what it is today without the nuclear family as the building block. So why is the family under attack as never before?

Today some would require the elimination of the family structure where parents are accountable to God and children accountable to parents. Today, Western Civilization has been seduced by some who make a mockery of the family:

- By persuading us "alternate lifestyles" are just as good as the institution of marriage;
- By persuading us the state should take the central role in educating children;
- By persuading us the killing of unborn children is a valid choice for pregnant women and should be supported by tax subsidies;
- By persuading us both parents should be employed;
- By persuading us small children develop just as well when cared for by strangers in group situations as they do when raised by parents;
- By sexualizing our children at younger ages;
- By convincing us there is nothing we can do about the increasingly high divorce rate in this country and that divorce does not necessarily hurt children.

The traditional family is under attack.

"The family in America today is undeniably weaker than at any point in our nation's history. One child in four today is born out of wedlock. One child in two spends at least part of his childhood in a single-parent household. One child in five lives in a family receiving some form of public assistance."
—*Pat Robertson*

Family matters because it is the single most outcome-determinative factor shaping our outlook and achievement. Our family powerfully determines what we become and how we think about ourselves, and so it will be for our children. That is why among all words in the English language, none means more to human beings than "family." Sadly, the words "husband," "wife," and "family" are being edited out of all American history and social studies school textbooks.

What anecdotes suggest, research confirms: Over the last four decades, marriage and family life have undergone an extraordinary transformation, yielding arrangements as temporary and as fragile—and as widespread—as those detailed above. "The scale of marital breakdown in the West since 1960 has no historical precedent and seems unique," exclaims the distinguished historian Lawrence Stone. At no time in history, with the possible exception of Imperial Rome, has the institution of marriage been more problematic than it is today," adds the demographer Kingsley Davis. In the judgment of James Q. Wilson, America's preeminent social scientist, we are witnessing a "profound, world-wide, long-term change in the family that is likely to continue for a long time."
—*William J. Bennett*[2]

Cynics will tell us that in our fast-paced society, "family" is becoming obsolete. They declare that family is an old-fashioned, lost concept, getting buried in a busy world of enlightened people. This is a fight we can and must win.

As a parent you have the power to set your child on a course for success. You may or may not feel powerful right now, but if you have the courage to rise to the challenge, your child can and will be blessed beyond belief.

Same-sex "marriage" is simply a ruse. The real agenda of its advocates is to deconstruct marriage. Radical lesbian activist and University of Michigan Law Professor Paula Ettelbrick declares to our society:

Being queer means pushing the parameters of sex, sexuality, and family, and in the process **transforming the very fabric of society**.... We must keep our eyes on the goals of providing true alternatives to marriage and of radically reordering society's view of family.[3]

Censoring Public School Textbooks

Beginning in the early 1980s, America's public school system has been used by social planners to change minds and hearts. Christians, for the most part, have been oblivious to what has been occuring. There has been a conscious "dumbing down" of public education since the 1920s, the emphasis shifting from the academic to a thoroughly embedded effort to move young minds away from traditional values.

Schools are succeeding at the following:

- Altering moral values
- Celebrating diversity to change lifestyles
- Undermining patriotism
- Fostering dependence on government
- Denigrating free enterprise

Public school textbooks are fertile ground for willful and historical deception. In Paul C. Vitz's study of textbooks from the first to the fourth grade, used to introduce children to U.S. society, family life, community activities and history, none of the books

contained one word referring to any religious activity in contemporary American life.[4] Evidence that religion has been cleansed from the public school curriculum abounds.[5]

Some particular examples of the bias against religion are significant. One social studies book has 30 pages on the Pilgrims, including the first Thanksgiving, but there is not one word that referred to religion as being a part of the Pilgrims' lives. One mother whose son is in a class using this book wrote me to say that he came home and told her that "**Thanksgiving was when the Pilgrims gave thanks to the Indians**." The mother called the principal of his suburban New York City school to point out that Thanksgiving was when the Pilgrims thanked God. The principal responded by saying that was her opinion but "the schools could only teach what was in the books."

In 1986, school children in Seattle, Washington, were given a dose of revisionist history in the booklet, "Teaching About Thanksgiving." The children were told, "The Pilgrims were **narrow-minded bigots who survived initially only with the Indians' help**, but turned on them when their help wasn't needed anymore."

American public school history books throughout the nation rarely quote from the parts of the Mayflower Compact that mention God. Most books cite it as a mere political document and delete the religious elements. Critics of America's early Christian origins have steadily removed references from textbooks and created a tense, legal environment that frightens many teachers from even raising evidence contradicting the text.

Early American textbooks referred to God without embarrassment. Public schools considered the development of character through the teaching of religion to be one of their major tasks.

Noah Webster

"The education of youth [is] an employment of more consequence than making laws and preaching the gospel, because it lays the foundation on which both law and gospel rest for success."
—Noah Webster, *American Magazine,* March 1780

The direction our nation has been going in the last few decades is a direct result of the training our present government leaders received during their years in school. Webster, the "Father of American Scholarship and Education," knew the importance of giving our children a good, solid education.

Webster developed a number of textbooks and reference books which became the standard for learning for well over a century. His *Blue-Backed Speller* sold over 100 million copies from 1783

The Elementary Spelling Book a.k.a. The Blue-Backed Speller

through the 1800s and was designed to allow students to be self-taught. His dictionary (1828) was the first of its kind to be published in the United States. Webster spent twenty-six years working on this exhaustive collection of words and definitions and often defined words biblically with the use of scriptural references.

In the 1970 Edition of *Webster's Collegiate Dictionary,* the word "educate" is defined as "to develop mentally and morally, especially by instruction." This classic meaning of education is to train the minds and morals of students and impart the moral and intellectual heritage of our culture. When the Constitution was written, Christian religious instruction was the primary purpose of education.

The Northwest Ordinance (1789), one of three founding documents of the United States, reminds us:

Creationism cannot be taught in our public schools.

"Religion, morality, and knowledge, being necessary to good government and the happiness of mankind, schools and the meaning of education shall forever be encouraged."

Unfortunately, in the arsenal of today's liberal educators, psychological manipulation and destruction of religious faith result in scarcely any facts being imparted and absolutely no morality. Moral instruction grows weaker.

Denial of the value of Western tradition and the repudiation of the role of religion in our past accompany the moral and academic decline in America. Some educators are moved not only by denial of the existence of God but militant hostility to any form of Judeo-Christian theism. *Creationism* cannot be taught because it requires a belief in God, *morality* cannot be taught because it requires a reference for the Word of God, and *history* cannot be taught without major revisions because our entire history speaks of the importance of God and religious values throughout the entire record of human affairs.[6]

In Webster's view, the central goal of education was to train youth in the precepts of Christianity. In a letter to David McClure in 1836, Webster stated:

"In my view, the Christian religion is the most important and one of the first things in which all children, under a free government, ought to be instructed.... No truth is more evident to my mind than the Christian religion must be the basis of any government intended to secure the rights and privileges of a free people."

Historical facts pose an enormous problem for secular liberals. How can they explain America without getting into the area of religion? The answer is that they cannot accurately teach or deal with American history without recognizing religion as a central reality, so they simply ignore the topic.

If they do not teach about the Founding Fathers, they do not have to teach about our Creator. If they do not teach about Abraham Lincoln, they do not have to deal with 14 references to God and the two Bible verses in his 732-word Second Inaugural Address. Abraham Lincoln said, "The philosophy in the school room in one generation will be the philosophy of the government in the next."

It is one thing to prohibit public schools from endorsing religion, but does that mean all references on Christian influences in our history should be expunged from our textbooks? Despite the fact that Federal law is clear that schools may teach about religion, there has been a conscious decision to sanitize history textbooks of information concerning the dominant presence of Christianity in colonial culture.

Noah Webster stated in his "History of the United States" (1832):

"Almost all the civil liberty now enjoyed in the world owes its origin to the principles of the Christian religion ... the religion of Christ and His Apostles. This is genuine Christianity, and to this we owe our free constitutions of government."

The New Jersey Department of Education removed references to the Pilgrims and the Mayflower from its historical standards for school textbooks because "Pilgrim" suggested religion.

Professor Paul Vitz documented the purging of religion from public school textbooks, examining 60 widely used social studies textbooks used by 87 percent of all public school students. There wasn't one that imparted the spirituality of the Pilgrims.

"Religion, traditional family values, and many conservative positions have been reliably excluded from children's textbooks.... There is not one story or article in all these books in which the central motivation or major content is connected to Judeo-Christian religion..... None of the books covering grades one through four contain one word referring to any religious activity in contemporary American life."[7]

A study of our early textbooks reveals that religion played a major role:

Textbooks referred to God without embarrassment, and the public schools considered one of their major tasks the development of character through the teaching of religion. For example, The New England Primer opened with religious admonitions followed by the Lord's Prayer, the Apostle's Creed, the Ten Commandments, and the names of the books of the Bible.

A widely used textbook from 1836 to 1920 (more than 120 million sold) was *McGuffey's Eclectic Readers.* McGuffey stressed religion and its relationship to morality. The textbook did not question the truths of the Bible or their relevance to everyday contact and were "filled with stories from the Bible."[8]

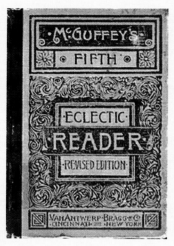

McGuffey's Eclectic Reader

Secular historians are steadily chipping away at the historical record, denying the impact Christianity has had on our nation. Books only have a scant or apologetic mention—either a fatal oversight or a deliberate purpose, and both alike to be deplored and condemned. A nation ashamed of its ancestry will be despised by its posterity.

Famed columnist Cal Thomas wrote:

"Public education is the training ground, the hothouse, the farm team for the next generation of liberals. How else to inculcate multiculturalism, political correctness and historical revisionism into children? How else to drum into them the view that they evolved from slime, that sex is an intramural sport and that the liberal agenda is best? Children might not be expected to encounter these "truths" on their own and are less likely to learn them in private schools, especially, religious schools where a real education, a moral conscience and wisdom can still be found."

Even the liberal "People for the American Way" acknowledged that religion is overlooked in our history books:

"Religion is simply not treated as a significant element in American life—it is not portrayed as an integrated part of the American value system or as something that is important to individual Americans."

A recent government study concluded that religion "was foolishly purged from many recent textbooks."[9] Although America's Christian heritage is being wiped clean, it is not too late to recover our nation's Christian past. There must be a renewed spirit to reestablish what has been forgotten and lost.

How we educate the current generation of youth will determine how our nation will be governed in the next generation. The education of our youth is so important.[10]

School Prayer

In 1963, the U.S. Supreme Court declared prayer to be an unconstitutional establishment of a religion. Isn't it a shame that we've taken prayer out of our schools and then been forced to install metal detectors? Immorality is robbing our children of their innocence. What happened to the day in our nation when we didn't have to have guards at school to prevent mass school murders or worry about the kids playing in the neighborhood? Could this be the effect of taking God out of our lives?

Without our belief in God, there is no foundation for our belief in the unalienable rights given by God. Our forefathers risked their lives, honors, and fortunes to preserve what Americans believe to be the rights of every man and woman—the right to life, liberty, and the pursuit of happiness. Our children have the constitutional right to share in that belief—the belief that gave birth to our great nation.

"I know that some believe that voluntary prayer in schools should be restricted to a moment of silence. We already have the right to remain silent—we can take our Fifth Amendment." *—**Ronald Reagan, 1984,** 40th President of the United States*

The Pledge of Allegiance
The founders of this nation based a national philosophy on a belief in God. The Declaration of Independence and the Bill of Rights locate inalienable rights in a Creator

rather than in government precisely so that such rights cannot be stripped away by government. In 1782, Thomas Jefferson wrote:

"Can the liberties of a nation be thought secure when we have removed their only firm basis, a conviction in the minds of the people that these liberties are the gift of God? That they are not to be violated by with His wrath?"

On many occasions George Washington acknowledged the role of divine providence in the nation's affairs. His first inaugural address is replete with references to God, including thanksgivings and supplications. In Washington's "Proclamation of a Day of National Thanksgiving," he wrote that it is the **"duty of all nations to acknowledge the providence of Almighty God, to obey His will, to be grateful for His benefits, and humbly to implore His protection and favor."** Washington used the phrase "under God" in his orders to the Continental Army. He wrote, "The fate of unborn millions will now depend, under God, on the courage and conduct of this army." The founders may have differed over the contours of the relationship between religion and government, but they never deviated from the conviction that "there was a necessary and valuable moral connection between the two."

The Pledge of Allegiance is something every school child knows how to recite and was written in 1892:

"One nation under God" was added to the pledge in 1954.

I pledge allegiance to the flag of the United States of America and to the Republic for which it stands, one nation under God, indivisible, with liberty and justice for all.

The 1954 addition of the phrase "one nation under God" in the Pledge of Allegiance simply decries an indisputable historical fact. As one commentator has observed,

> "The Pledge [of Allegiance] accurately reflects how the founding generation viewed the separation of powers as the surest security of civil right. Anchoring basic rights upon a metaphysical source is very much part of that structural separation, for without God, the law is invited to become god. This was well known to Rousseau and Marx who both complained that acknowledging God creates a competition or check upon the secular state."

The U.S. Supreme court recognized the primacy of religion in the nation's heritage in *Zorach v. Clauson* (1952):

> "**We are a religious people whose institutions presuppose a Supreme Being**.... When the state encourages religious instruction or cooperates with religious authorities by adjusting the schedule of public events to sectarian needs, it follows the best of our traditions. For it then respects the religious nature of our people and accommodates the public service to their spiritual needs. To hold that it may not would be to find in the Constitution a requirement that the government show a callous indifference to religious groups. That would be preferring those who believe in no religion over those who do believe."
> —*Justice William O. Douglas*

Public acknowledgments of God are under attack by groups bent on rewriting American history and removing religion from the public square. These groups try to convince Americans that public acknowledgments of God establish a national religion. They ignore the fact that from colonial times to the present, historical documents and governmental leaders repeatedly acknowledged God. There is a huge difference between public acknowledgment of God and an establishment of religion. While the latter is forbidden by the United States Constitution, the former is as American as it is patriotic.

United States Supreme Court Justice Warren Burger, writing for the majority observed that "Our history is replete with official references to the value and invocation of divine guidance...."

Patriotic Songs

All our traditional hymns of praise of the United States conspicuously mention God. Our national anthem, *The Star Spangled Banner,* includes Francis Scott Key's religious sentiments in its final verse "... and this be our motto: In God is our Trust." *America the Beautiful* features a chorus with the cherished words, "America, America, God shed His grace on thee." Surely this must offend secularists.

"America, My Country 'Tis Of Thee" has the inescapable verses:

Our Father's God to Thee
Author of liberty,
To Thee we sing.
Long may our land be bright.
With freedom's holy light;
Protect us from Thy might,
Great God, our King.

The Battle Hymn of the Republic isn't just merely religious, it's specifically Christian. The word, "Hallelujah" means "Praise the name of God" in Hebrew. Julia Ward Howe's song was a proselytizing instrument whose assumption of Christian commitment in soldiers and the nation made it a powerful inducement to Christian adherence and practice.

Francis Scott Key wrote "The Star Spangled Banner."

I have seen Him in the watch-
fires of a hundred circling camps;
They have builded Him an altar in the evening dews and damps;
I have read His righteous sentence by the dim and flaring lamps;
His day is marching on.

I have read a fiery gospel, writ in burnished rows of steel,
As ye deal with my condemners, so with you my grace shall deal;
Let the Hero, born on woman, crush the serpent with His heel,
Since God is marching on.

These songs indicate the intermixing on nationalism and religion which go back to the beginning of the Republic.

If secularists intend to shape a new sense of American identify stripped of religious and Christian trappings, they had better get to work in composing a fresh array of new patriotic songs.

Christian Oaths

The American colonists adopted English test oaths to support Anglican congregations. State constitutions during the war commonly required test oaths for holding public office. Only Protestants could hold public office in New Jersey or sit in the legislatures of Georgia, South Carolina, and New Hampshire. Only those professing "the Christian religion" could hold public office or serve in high government positions in Massachusetts.

North Carolina limited public offices to those who believed in God, the truth of the Protestant religion, and the divine authority of both the Old and New Testaments. Quakers recited religious texts before taking their seats. Pennsylvania Legislators had to declare:

"I do believe in one God, the Creator and Governor of the Universe, the rewarder of the good and the punisher of the wicked. And I do acknowledge the Scriptures of the Old and New Testament to be given by Divine inspiration."

Delaware went further by requiring all office holders to profess belief in the Trinity and the divine inspiration of the Bible. Today, all courts of law, state and federal, require an oath before testifying with the option to use the word "affirm" rather than "swear." Hundreds of other various statutes such as entering the military, naturalization, and tax forms, all require various forms of oaths (So help me, God).

OATH OF ALLEGIANCE
I hereby declare, on oath, that I absolutely and entirely renounce and abjure all allegiance and fidelity to any foreign prince, potentate, state, or sovereignty, of whom or which I have heretofore been a subject or citizen; that I will support and defend the Constitution and laws of the United States of America against all enemies, foreign and domestic; that I will bear true faith and allegiance to the same; that I will bear arms on behalf of the United Stated which required by the law; that I will perform noncombatant service in the Armed Forces of the United States when required by the law; that I will perform work of national importance under civilian direction when required by the law; and that I will take this obligation freely, without any mental reservation or purposes of evasion; so help me God.

The American Civil Liberties Union

Effective organizations for destroying the laws, morals, and traditional rights of Americans have been People for the American Way, Americans United for Separation of Church and State, American Atheists, and Freedom from Religion Foundation—all like-minded organizations of the ACLU. Founded in 1920, the ACLU is the legal arm of the humanist movement, established and nurtured by the ethical culture movement.[11] Founders of the ACLU include William Z. Foster (formerly the head of the United States Communist Party) and Roger Baldwin (conscientious objector and convicted felon).

After ten years under the directorship of Baldwin, the ACLU was probed in the early 1930s by the United States House of Representatives special committee to investigate communist activities in the United States. On January 17, 1931, the Committee Report stated:

> "The American Civil Liberties Union is closely affiliated with the communist movement in the United States, and fully 90 percent of its efforts are on behalf of communists who have come into conflict with the law. It claims to stand for free speech, free press, and free assembly, but it is quite apparent that the main function of the ACLU is to attempt to protect the communists in their advocacy of force and violence to overthrow the Government, replacing the American flag by a red flag and erecting a Soviet Government in place of the republican form of government guaranteed to each State by the Federal Constitution."[12]

Activities of the ACLU will sound familiar to anyone conversant with the events of the past few decades:

- Legal defense to support Fidel Castro
- Same sex marriages
- Opposition to voluntary prayer and Bible reading in public schools
- Antagonism toward laws which control subversive organizations
- Efforts to delete the words "under God" from the Pledge of Allegiance
- Opposition to state narcotics laws
- Legalization of child pornography
- Legalization of all drugs
- Support abolition of monogamy laws

The ACLU seeks to ban the Ten Commandments and any other reference to God from the public square. They relentlessly attack traditional values including marriage and have vowed to impose same sex "marriage" on our nation through the courts because it has failed at the ballot box.

The ACLU and its allies have been very effective in advancing their radical and destructive ideology:

> The ACLU's dream of changing our nation advanced at an incredible pace. In less than 100 years, it has changed much about American law on the issues that most effect our national character.... The ACLU succeeded not only because it pursued its goals so relentlessly, but especially because few stood in its way.

The ACLU participates in thousands of cases each year. Occasionally, it defends the Constitutional Rights of radical right-wing organizations such as the Ku Klux Klan, but only so they can claim to represent persons from both sides of the political spectrum. Enjoying some court victories, the ACLU has asked their supporters to hunt down every display of the Ten Commandments for the purpose of eradicating them by judicial action.

The ACLU debases itself by supporting immoral causes such as prostitution, homosexual behavior, and kiddy porn.

"I am for socialism, disarmament, and ultimately the abolishing of the state itself as an instrument of violence and compulsion. I seek special ownership of property, the abolition of the propertied class, and sole control by those who produce wealth. Communism is the goal."

—Roger Baldwin, ACLU Founder (1935)[13]

Goals of the ACLU:
- Force the Ten Commandments to be expunged from the U.S. Supreme Court Building and all other public buildings in America;
- Require the U.S. House and Senate to fire its chaplains;
- Remove "Under God" from the Pledge of Allegiance;
- Remove all crosses and Stars of David from the gravestones of American soldiers in military cemeteries around the world;
- Obtain major revisions and deletions in the public use of all American historical documents;

- Take "signed in 1787 in the year of our Lord" out of our Constitution;
- Remove "In God We Trust" from all coins;
- Delete the word God from "My Country 'Tis of Thee" and "The Star Spangled Banner";
- Chisel out the words "known but to God" from the Tomb of the Unknown Soldier;
- Declare all legal prohibitions on the distribution of obscene material—including child pornography—as unconstitutional;[14]
- Let pornographic outlets locate wherever they please—whether next to churches or day-care centers or near residential neighborhoods;[15]
- Do not restrict access of children to pornography on the Internet in tax-funded libraries;[16]
- Do not give legal recourse to parents when it comes to shielding their children from exposure to hard-core pornography;[17]
- Do not allow the military to stop open displays of homosexual behavior within its ranks;[18]
- Do not allow parents to limit their children's exposure to or participation in public school classes and assemblies, any topic—except Orthodox Jewish or Christian teachings—that violates the family's core religious and moral beliefs;[19]
- Do not allow public schools to observe recognized religious, historical, and cultural holidays such as Christmas, Easter, or Hanukkah;[20]
- Abolish all legislative, military, and prison chaplaincy programs;[21]
- Abolish all criminal and civil laws that prohibit polygamy (having multiple wives)[22] and same-sex "marriage."[23]

"Society is defining deviancy downward. We are becoming numb to acts that once shocked us, inviting a deeper level of depravity."
—*The late Patrick Moynihan, United States Senate, (D-NY) (1999)*

The Battle Over the Motto

The phrases, "In God We Trust," "So Help Me God," "Under God," "The Year of Our Lord," and similar invocations were commonplace in America even before Washington. In the early days of the Civil War, Treasury Secretary Salmon P. Chase instructed the director of the U.S. Mint to prepare a motto for the nation's coins.

"Dear Sir," his memo began: "No nation can be strong except in the strength of God, or safe except in His defense. The trust of our people in God should be declared on our national coins." In 1861, Pennsylvania minister Rev. M. R. Watkinson wrote Treasury Secretary Salmon P. Chase suggesting "the recognition of the Almighty God in some form on our coins ... it would place us openly under the Divine protection we have personally claimed." Chase agreed and ordered that "In God We Trust" appear on U.S. coins. And so, "In God We Trust" first appeared on the 1864 two-cent coin.

After Congress passed the necessary legislation in 1856, it became the official motto, but it has been our informal national motto for nearly 150 years. It captures the essence of the American people's firm belief in God since the earliest colonial days.

Religious statements about God were printed on American coins as far back as 1694, when the colony of Carolina printed "God preserve Carolina and the Lord's Proprietors" on a one-cent piece. A New England token printed that same year bore the inscription "God preserve New England."[24] Louisiana minted a coin in 1721 that carried the words "Holiness of the Lord."[25]

To the Founders and succeeding generations, it

The motto "In God We Trust" has been moved from the face of our new $1 coins to the edge—nearly invisible!

must have seemed inconceivable that expressions of Christian faith and public reliance on God would ever be anything than commonly accepted and practiced as a constant reminder of our foundations and the source of our strength and blessings.

Legislative Prayer

Prayer is deeply imbedded in the history and tradition of this country. From colonial times through the founding of the Republic and ever since, the practice of legislative prayer has co-existed with religious freedom.

The men who wrote the First Amendment did not view paid legislative chaplains and opening prayers as a violation of that Amendment, for the practice of opening sessions with prayer continues without interruption ever since that early session of Congress. It has also been followed consistently in most of the states.

In 1983, approving the practice, the U.S. Supreme Court ruled:

"The practice of opening sessions of Congress with prayer has continued without interruption for almost 200 years ever since the first congress drafted the First Amendment ... [such] historical evidence sheds light not only what the drafters of the First Amendment intended the Establishment Clause to mean but also how they thought the Clause applied ... it would be incongruous to interpret the Clause as imposing more stringent First Amendment limits on the states than the draftsmen imposed on the Federal Government. In light of the history, there can be no doubt that the practice of opening Legislative sessions with prayer has become part of the fabric of our society. To invoke Divine guidance on a public body entrusted with making the laws is not a violation of the Establishment Clause; it is simply a tolerable acknowledgement of beliefs widely held among the people of this country."

First Prayer in Congress: From the official journals of the Continental Congress: September 6, 1774 resolved: That the Rev. Mr. Cuché be desired to open the Congress tomorrow morning with prayers. September 6, 1774 Voted: That the thanks of the Congress be given to the Rev. Duché ... for performing divine service, and for the excellent prayer which he composed and delivered on the occasion.

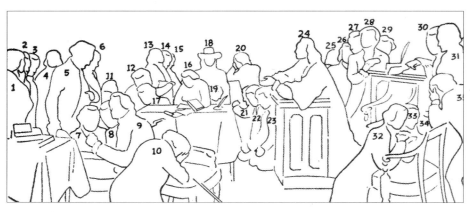

1. Cesar Rodney, DE	10. Peyton Randolph, VA	19. John Dehart, NJ	28. Samuel Chase, MD
2. Edward Rutledge, SC	11. Col. N. Folson, NH	20. William Livingston, NJ	29. John Morton, PA
3. T. Cushing, MA	12. Robert Paine, MA	21. Thomas McKean, DE	30. Thomas Mifflin, PA
4. Ephilet Dyer, CT	13. George Read, DE	22. Roger Sherman, CT	31. Charles Thompson, VA
5. John Adams, MA	14. Silas Dean, CT	23. William Paca, ND	32. Rich. Henry Lee, VA
6. John Adams, MA	15. Richard Smith, NJ	24. Rev. Mr. Duché, PA	33. John Jay, NY
7. Patrick Henry, VA	16. Philip Livingston, NY	25. Samuel Rhodes, PA	34. Isaac Low, NY
8. John Rutledge, SC	17. Thomas Lynch, SC	26. Col. William Floyd, NY	35. Benjamin Harrison, VA
9. George Washington, VA	18. Stephen Hopkins, RI	27. Stephen Crane, NJ	36. Samuel Ward, RI

✠

Chapter 9

Common Myths About Church and State

Until *Everson v. Board of Education* (1947)[1] the term "wall of separation of church and state" was seldom found in any document outside of an obscure letter written in 1802 by Thomas Jefferson.[2] His letter is only one of 100,000 documents penned by the Founding Fathers during this time. If we looked at all these letters and documents and tried to pull out one phrase or quotation it would be silly; however, that is what happened. Thus it is today that the First Amendment is manipulated to fit into the philosophical position which makes a mockery of the intent of the writers.

Current examples that totally disprove the lie that the Founding Fathers intended for there to be a separation of church and state include the following:

- The Pledge of Allegiance cites "One Nation Under God."
- All military branches of the United States pay chaplains.
- The inscription in a band around the top of the Liberty Bell cites Leviticus 25:10, "Proclaim liberty throughout all the land, unto the inhabitants thereof."
- A portrait of Moses with the Ten Commandments hangs in the United States Supreme Court.
- The words, "Judgments of the Lord are righteous," are chiseled on the Lincoln Memorial.
- There is a prayer room in the Capitol building.
- The Tomb of the Unknown Soldier is dedicated to a soldier "known but to God."

The U.S. Air Force Academy Chapel

- The United States Supreme Court opens with the words, "God save the United States and this Honorable Court." Courtroom witnesses swear to tell the truth, "So help me, God."
- The government mandated a National Day of Prayer.

- The government mandated Thanksgiving in which we're asked to give thanks unto God.
- The government acknowledges Christmas, as the birth of Jesus Christ, by federal law.
- The last stanza of the "Star Spangled Banner" refers to God.
- The Declaration of Independence refers to God four times.

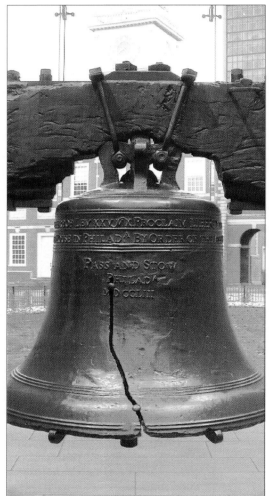

The Liberty Bell in Philadelphia

- Our calendar is dated from the year of the birth of Jesus Christ.
- Almost all states have constitutions or preambles that refer to God.
- Some of America's favorite patriotic songs, "Battle Hymn of the Republic," "America the Beautiful," "America," and "My Country 'Tis of Thee," refer to God.
- "In God We Trust" is inscribed on all our coins. An act of Congress, April 11, 1864, authorized this motto on coins. In May, 1908 "In God We Trust" was mandatory on all coins.
- The Constitution, signed in 1787, was "in the year of Our Lord."
- Moses, bearing the Ten Commandments, is pictured in the Library of Congress Rotunda.
- A stained glass window of George Washington on bended knee in prayer is in the prayer chapel in the U.S. Capitol.
- Depiction of the Ten Commandments resides on the floor of the National Archives.
- The "Liberty of Worship" statute rests on the Ten Commandments outside the Ronald Reagan Building.
- The Library of Congress rotunda bears a plaque with a phrase from Lord Tennyson: "One God, one law, one element, and one far off divine event to which the whole creation moves."
- The words "In God We Trust" are inscribed in the House and Senate chambers.

- The walls of the Capitol dome contain: "The New Testament according to the Lord and Savior Jesus Christ."
- There is a figure of the crucified Christ in the Capitol Rotunda.
- The painting, "The Baptism of Pocahontas at Jamestown," hangs in the Capitol Rotunda.
- The painting "Embarkation of the Pilgrims" in the Capital Rotunda shows Elder William Brewster holding a Bible opened to the title page which reads, "The New Testament of Our Lord and Savior Jesus Christ." The words "God With Us" are inscribed on the ship.
- The Latin phrase *Annuit Coeptis*, "[God] has smiled on our undertaking," is inscribed on the Great Seal of the United States.

The Baptism of Pocahontas in the Capitol Rotunda

- Under the Seal is the phrase from Lincoln's Gettysburg address: "This nation under God."
- President Eliot of Harvard chose Micah 6:8 for the walls of the Library of Congress: "He hath showed thee, O man, what is good; and what doth God require of thee, but to do justly, and to love mercy, and to walk humbly with thy God."
- The Lawmaker's Library quotes the psalmist's acknowledgment of the beauty and order of creation: "The heavens declare the glory of God, and the firmament showeth His handiwork" (Psalm 19:1).
- Engraved on the metal cap on the top of the Washington Monument are the words: "Praise be to God." Lining the walls of the stairwell are numerous Bible verses: "Search the Scriptures" (John 5:30), "Holiness to the Lord," and "Train up a child in the way he should go, and when he is old he will not depart from it" (Proverbs 22:6).

The Jefferson Memorial

- At the opposite end of the Lincoln Memorial, words and phrases from Lincoln's Second Inaugural Address allude to "God," "the Bible," "Providence," "the Almighty," and "Divine Attributes."
- A plaque in the Dirksen Office Building has the words, "In God We Trust" in bronze relief.
- On the Jefferson Memorial are the words, "God who gave us life Gave us liberty. Can the liberties of nation be secure when we have removed a conviction that these liberties are the gift of God? Indeed I tremble for my country when I reflect that God is just, that his justice cannot sleep forever."

Oath-taking Ceremony

- The Senate doors show George Washington taking the presidential oath with his hands on a Bible.
- The rotunda of the Capitol building includes paintings of George Washington ascending into heaven.
- The Cox corridor of the Capitol building is inscribed with Katharyn Lee Bates' hymn "America the Beautiful," which includes "America! God shed his grace on thee and crown thy good with brotherhood from sea to shining sea."
- In the prayer room of the House Chamber the following prayer is written "Preserve me, O God—for in thee do I put my trust."
- The U.S. Supreme Court in *Vidal v. Girard* (1844)[3] said it would never allow Christianity to be "maliciously and openly reviled and blasphemed against, to the annoyance of believers or the injury of the public."

True or False?

The U.S. Constitution creates a separation of church and state.

FALSE: The literal phrase "separation of church and state" does not appear in the Constitution, and it stretches the imagination to argue that the concept is there. The prohibition is that Congress (the federal government) shall not establish a religion but equally important the federal government may not "prohibit" the free exercise thereof. It is inappropriate to speak of the "constitutional principle of church and state separation" because it does not exist.

Thomas Jefferson's 1802 letter to the Danbury Baptist Church should be regarded as law.

FALSE: Historical archives contain thousands of letters and writings of our Founding Fathers. Many hundreds of those documents discuss that our nation was founded as a Christian nation, but only a sparse few claimed the law to have a "wall of separation."

The separation of church and state is found in the Constitution of the **Soviet Union**.

TRUE: The Soviet Constitution, Article 124 (1947) reads: "In order to ensure to citizens' freedom of conscience, **the church in the U.S.S.R. is separated from the state**, and the school from the church. Freedom of religious worship and freedom of antireligious propaganda is recognized for all citizens."

St. Basil's in Moscow

The United States was not founded as a Christian nation.

FALSE: The founding of the United States as a political unit with the settlement of North America included Europeans arriving on our shores seeking freedom to worship. Many believed they were establishing some type of Christian utopia and in fact, during the Constitutional Convention, a minority faction favored some recognition of Christianity in the Constitution.

Delegate Luther Martin in a report to Maryland lawmakers asserted many believed in "a Christian country, it would be at least decent to hold out some distinction between the professors of Christianity and downright infidelity or paganism."

The various colonies had state-sponsored Christian churches and most had requirements that running for public office required one to be a Christian and take an oath.

The Supreme Court has never declared that the U.S. is a Christian nation.

FALSE: In 1892, and in many other published decisions, the court stated "this is a Christian nation," an official court pronouncement that sets legally binding precedent cases stating the same principle.

Moses with the Ten Commandments

Early state constitutions contain language limiting public office to Christians.

TRUE: Our early state constitutions did limit public office to Christians for those who believed in heaven and hell when church and state were united.

The First Amendment's religion clause was intended to prevent the establishment of a national church.

TRUE: The Framers wanted to ban a national church, to ban not only the establishment of a single church but also multiple establishments.

Ever since prayer was removed from schools, public school performance has declined and social ills have increased.

TRUE: School performance has decreased since 1962, SAT scores are lower today, and there are many problems experienced in American society from the increase of teenage venereal disease, teenage pregnancies, divorce rate, juvenile delinquency, drug use, and abortions, which are all indicators of American society declining since 1962.

American law is not based on the Ten Commandments.

Public school performance has declined.

FALSE: Most of the Ten Commandments are included in American law such as murder, stealing, and lying.

Numerous U.S. Supreme Court cases and State Court cases have duly noted the Ten Commandments' rightful place in American legal history.

The acknowledgment of the Ten Commandments demonstrates that "our history is pervaded by expressions of religious beliefs."

The Ten Commandments did "have a significant impact on the development of secular legal codes of the Western World."

Twelve of the thirteen original colonies adopted the entire Decalogue in their civil and criminal laws.

The Founding Fathers wrote a godless constitution that does not refer to Jesus.

FALSE: The final line of the U.S. Constitution was signed in 1787 "in the year of our Lord," which clearly refers to Jesus having been born 1787 years earlier.

The U.S. Constitution clearly refers to the Declaration of Independence, which mentions God four times.

New laws are forbidden to become effective on the Sabbath.

The Declaration of Independence is a Deist document since it refers to the Creator.

FALSE: This misinformation is an example of revisionist crackpot history.

Either 52 or 53 of the drafters of the Declaration of Independence were Christian, and it is debatable about the other two.

Many writers of the liberal left, such as Robert Boston, spread misinformation such as this.

The ACLU was formed by an admitted Marxist.

TRUE: Roger Baldwin was a conscientious objector, convicted felon, and avowed Marxist.

The vast majority of Americans do not have a deep faith in God.

FALSE: Gallup Polls show over 90 percent of Americans believe in God and only two percent say they do not.

People's belief in heaven and angels is extremely high, over 80 percent.

Nearly 60 percent of all Americans say religion is "very important" in their life.

Nearly 65 percent say they believe religion can answer most of today's problems.

Massachusetts was one of the first states which believed in separation of church and state.

FALSE: Massachusetts levied a tax on all citizens to support religion and the clergy. Those who didn't pay went straight to jail, no questions asked. Ministers were kept under close control. Since ministers were paid by the government, any who rebelled were quickly replaced. In most of the other states, citizens were taxed to support the Protestant denomination of their choosing.

Separation of church and state existed in colonial America.

FALSE: As we understand that concept, it existed nowhere in colonial America. Citizens were taxed to support religion, strict Sunday laws were rigidly enforced, blasphemy was a capital offense, and candidates had to swear to support Christianity before they could hold public office.

Signing the U.S. Constitution

Thomas Jefferson put into practice a separation of church and state.

FALSE: There are many examples of Jefferson supporting the concept of using tax dollars for religion and attending church in our nation's Capitol.

National monuments are forbidden to mention God or Christ.

FALSE: Countless monuments bear inscriptions of the Bible and references to Jesus.

It is forbidden to teach the Bible or mention Jesus in public schools.

FALSE: Schools are allowed to instruct and refer to the Bible and Jesus in the context of world and national history.

It is forbidden to sing Christmas songs in public schools.

FALSE: Christmas songs reflect a cultural and traditional holiday and may be sung.

No tax dollars are permitted to be given to corporate church schools.

FALSE: As long as the primary purpose is secular and not religious, public money may be used.

The Judeo-Christian Ethic

Today we can accurately describe the general principles of Christianity as the "Judeo-Christian Ethic" since the Founders showed great attachment to the Hebrews.

John Witherspoon wrote:

> "To the Jews were first committed the care of the sacred writings … yet was the providence of God particularly manifest in their preservation and purity. The Jews were so faithful in their important trust."

Elias Boudinot, President of Congress in 1782-83, made personal provisions to bring persecuted Jews to America where they could find safety.

John Adams wrote:

> "I will insist that the Hebrews have done more to civilize men than any other nation. They preserve and propagate to all mankind the doctrine of a supreme, intelligent, wise, almighty Sovereign of the Universe, which I believe to be the great essential principle of all morality, and consequently of all civilization."

Rabbi Daniel Lapin defends American Christian conservatives:

John Witherspoon

> "I desperately want my children to have the option of living peacefully and productively in the United States of America. I am certain this depends upon America regaining its Christian-oriented moral compass … in defending Christianity in America, I'm not suggesting that Jews are to embrace the Christian faith … but I am suggesting at the very least, the Jews should stop speaking and acting as if Christian America is their enemy."

The United States is the most religious of all Western democracies and is religiously diverse. The Immigration Act of 1965 eliminated quotas linked to national origin and Muslims, Buddhists, Hindus, Sikhs, and others have arrived in increasing numbers. These diverse religions are no longer only on the other side of the world but in our own neighborhoods. Though the numbers of non-Christians are relatively small (about 6.5 percent of the U.S. population) their visibility and influence is growing.

"It is my earnest hope ... that from this solemn occasion, a better world shall emerge ... a world dedicated to the dignity of man ... Let us pray that peace be restored to the world, and that God will preserve it always."
—*General Douglas MacArthur, 1946*

Gen. Douglas MacArthur

"Each period of our national history has had its special challenges. Those that confront us now are as momentous as any in the past. Today marks the beginning not only of a new administration, but of a period that will be eventful, perhaps decisive, for us and for the world.

"It is fitting, therefore, that we take this occasion to proclaim to the world the essential principles of the faith by which we live, and to declare our aims to all peoples. The American people stand firm in the faith which has inspired this nation from the beginning. We believe that all men have a right to equal justice under law and equal opportunity to share in the common good. We believe that all men have a right to freedom of thought and expression. We believe that all men are created equal because they are created in the image of God. From this faith we will not be moved ... to that end we will devote our strength, our resources, and our firmness of resolve. With God's help, the future of mankind will be assured in a world of justice, harmony, and peace."
—*Harry S Truman, Inaugural Address, January 20, 1949*

President Harry S Truman

Political Correctness

Political correctness is a tool of those who would attempt to change life in America as defined in the Constitution. The political left has tried to redefine family and patriotism among other clearly evident concepts: to make them conform to their own perverse worldview, all under the guise of political correctness. The churches are silent while the courts legislate immorality. Extreme liberalism seeks to dismantle our border, language, and culture.[4]

- The YWCA once hired Patricia Ireland, a bisexual, proabortion feminist, to head the 145-year-old, Christian-based young girls' association.

- The United Way de-funded more than fifty Boy Scouts of America chapters over the Scouts' refusal to offer special homosexual counseling for gay youth.[5]

- Princeton University advocates the murder of disabled babies for up to several weeks after they have been born.

- The term, "Founding Fathers," is out, replaced by the term, the "Framers." The feminists say this new generic label in textbooks will be less sexist and more tolerant.

- The word "marriage" is old-fashioned. To promote homosexuality, the new term is "union."

- The leading psychiatric groups such as the American Psychiatric Association are contemplating the normalization of pedophilia—sex with children.[6]

- An appellate court rules that forcing the recitation of the Pledge of Allegiance by students is unconstitutional. The inclusion of "under God" is offensive to atheists.

- The Court says anti-sodomy laws "demean" people. But doesn't legalizing sodomy demean our culture even more? The U.S. Supreme Court has legalized sodomy.

In communities throughout the country, the ACLU is fighting to expunge all signs of faith:

- They have threatened the National Parks Service in order to remove three small bronze plaques, each bearing a Bible verse, from a display in the Grand Canyon National Park.

- They fought and successfully prevented the Boy Scouts of America from maintaining their 50-year-old lease of Camp Balboa in San Diego over the Scouts' policy regarding homosexuals and their core belief in God.

- They asked the Virginia Supreme Court to legalize cross burning on public property. In their view, the current state ban suppresses the freedom of speech for the Ku Klux Klan and like-minded pyromaniacs.

- They are fighting to prevent students from reciting the Pledge of Allegiance at various public schools.

- They defend the North American Man Boy Love Association (NAMBLA), a despicable group of child molesters. NAMBLA publishes pedophilia propaganda: "Call it love, call it lust, call it whatever you want. We desire sex with boys, and boys, whether society is willing to admit it, desire sex with us."

- A federal court ruled it unconstitutional for a public cemetery to have a planter in the shape of a cross, since, as the court explained, the mere sight of it could cause "emotional distress" to a passerby and thus constitute "injury-in-fact."

- A federal court ruled a schoolteacher couldn't be seen in school with his own personal Bible, and a classroom library containing 237 books must remove the two titles dealing with Christianity.

- Convicted and sentenced by a jury for brutally clubbing to death a 71-year-old woman with an axe handle so he could steal her Social Security check, the perpetrator got his sentence overturned because the prosecuting attorney, in a statement lasting less than five seconds, mentioned a Bible verse in the courtroom.

Robert Kennedy's grave at Arlington

New American Meanings for Old Words

- God says, "Thou shalt not kill." Americans gave murder a new name and abort over 4,000 unborn babies each day.
- God calls it "drunkenness." We call it "alcoholism—a social disease."
- God calls it "sodomy." We call it "gay rights, an alternative lifestyle."
- God calls it "perversion." We call it "adult entertainment."
- God calls it "immorality." We call it the "new morality."
- God calls it "cheating." We call it "abnormal social development."
- What was once "welfare" is now "government entitlement."
- What was once "divorce" is now "dissolution of marriage."

Understanding the First Amendment

When the Constitution was sent to the states for ratification, there was fear it would give the new national government too much power. It was proposed that specific prohibitions should be listed in the Constitution to add further restrictions on the national government's power and jurisdiction.

The area of religion was important since most of the states had established churches that were supported with taxes. There was concern that a national church (i.e., Anglican, Presbyterian, or Congregational) would be funded by tax dollars, thereby disestablishing the different religious expressions in the various state constitutions. Therefore, the First Amendment was designed to protect the states against the very thing that is happening today—a federalization of issues related to religion. The amendment was not designed to disestablish the Christian religion, which was predominant in the colonies. Justice Joseph Story (1779-1845), a Supreme Court justice of the 19th century, offers the following commentary on the amendment's meaning:

> "The real object of the First Amendment was not to countenance, much less to advance Mohammedanism, or Judaism, or infidelity, by prostrating Christianity, but to exclude all rivalry among Christian sects [denominations] and to prevent any national ecclesiastical establishment which would give to an hierarchy the exclusive patronage of the national government."

Story's comments are important. The Amendment's purpose was "to exclude all rivalry among Christian sects." This presupposes Christianity was the accepted religion of the colonies but that no single denomination should be supported by the national government. The Amendment was not designed to make all religions equal by excluding everything religious.

The Amendment prohibits not the establishment of religion by Congress (religion in general) but an establishment of religion (a Christian denomination in particular). Nothing in the First Amendment restrictied the states from establishing a religious sect.

If the Amendment was constructed to remove religion from having even the slightest impact on civil governmental issues, then it seems rather strange that on September 24, 1789, the same day that

Justice Joseph Story

Congress approved the First Amendment, it called on President Washington to proclaim a National Day of Prayer and Thanksgiving. These men had supposedly just separated religion from government at all levels, a government they would not have had if God had not made it possible.

The first Congress also established the congressional chaplain system by which official daily prayers to God are still offered. In the entire debate on the First Amendment, not one word was said by any Congressman about a "wall of separation between church and state." At the time of the drafting of the First Amendment, a number of the thirteen colonies had established churches.

At the beginning of the Revolution, established churches existed in nine of the colonies. The First Amendment in large part was a guarantee to the states, which insured that the states would be able to continue whatever church-state relationship existed in 1791. Maryland, Virginia, North Carolina, South Carolina, and Georgia all shared Anglicanism as the established religion common to those colonies. Congregationalism was the established religion in Massachusetts, New Hampshire, and Connecticut. New York allowed for the establishment of Protestant religions. Only in Rhode Island and Virginia were all religious sects disestablished. But all states still retained the Christian religion as the foundation of their social, civil, and political institutions. Rhode Island and Virginia continued to respect and acknowledge the Christian religion in their system of law.

Older versions of state constitutions were explicit about the Christian faith. For example, up until it was changed in 1876, North Carolina's Constitution read:

> "That no person who shall deny the being of God, or the truth of the Protestant religion, or the divine authority of the Old or New Testaments, or who shall hold religious principles incompatible with the freedom and safety of the State, shall be capable of holding any office or place of trust or profit in the civil department within this State."

As constitutional scholar Leo Pfeffer writes, "For all practical purposes Christianity and religion were synonymous."[7]

In *Lemon v. Kurtzman* (1971), the Supreme Court established a three-part test for deciding legal challenges to government practices that purportedly "establish" religion. The Lemon test[8] requires the Court to strike down laws appearing to promote or aid religion unless it determines that (1) the government action had a secular purpose, (2) the government action's primary effect is not to advance religion, and (3) the action does not foster an "excessive entanglement" with religion.[9] The Lemon test has been fiercely criticized by many legal scholars and even current Supreme Court justices for tipping the scales against religion. These critics argue, among other things, that the Constitution does not forbid government from "advancing" religion generally, so long as it does not "play favorites" between various religions. Lately, the Lemon test has fallen into such disrepute that the Court sometimes ignores it altogether.

The court used the Lemon test in the 2005 Ten Commandment cases, holding that the Ten Commandment displays may not create coercive pressure on individuals to participate in religion and must be intended primarily for a secular purpose.

The Framers had a clear understanding of these clauses: to forbid the federal government from setting up a national church and to prohibit the federal government from interfering with the church/state relations of the individual states.[10] Thus, Congress was prevented from interfering with the established churches in the states.

Supreme Court Chief Justice Story in his "Commentary on the Constitution of the United States" affirmed this point:

> "Thus, the whole power over the subject of religion was left exclusively to State governments, to be acted on according to their own sense of judgment and the State Constitutions."

Court rulings that the Establishment Clause prohibits invocations and benedictions at public school graduation ceremonies lay waste a tradition that is as old as public school graduation ceremonies themselves, and that is a component of an even more longstanding American tradition of nonsectarian prayer to God at public celebrations generally.

> "Read it! It says, 'Congress shall make no law respecting an establishment of religion or prohibiting the free exercise thereof.' Where is the word 'separate'? Where are the words 'church' or 'state'?
>
> "They are not there. Never have been. Never intended to be. Read the Congressional Records during that four-month period in 1789 when the amendment was being framed in Congress. Clearly their intent was to prohibit a single denomination in exclusion of all others, whether it was Anglican or Catholic or some other.
>
> "So, as the sand empties through my hourglass at warp speed—and with my time running out in this Senate and on this earth, I feel compelled to speak out. For I truly believe that at times like this, silence is not golden. It is yellow."
>
> —*Former U.S. Senator (D-GA) Zell Miller (2005)*[11]

Valedictorian Prayer

Federal courts have forbidden voluntary prayer in public schools and student-sponsored prayer at athletic events—even though the state isn't endorsing a particular religion or requiring students to participate. The long arm of the federal government, in its zeal to prevent an establishment of religion, now interferes with the free exercise of individuals; thus the establishment and free exercise clauses are often in full conflict. In the name of preventing the establishment of religion (erroneously referred to as upholding the separation of church and state, which was intended to promote, not restrict religious freedom), courts suppress the free exercise rights of individuals, students, and adults alike. This is precisely the kind of authoritarian tyranny the Founders sought to avoid.[12]

Christians will be forced to take a stand for Christ in our time as never before in American history. But as we take that stand, we must take care to take the right stand, in the right way, and with the right spirit. Christians must see that our responsibility to government is a responsibility as to God. That is what biblical submission to government is about.

Christians in America should not despair. Our hope is in Christ, and we are merely pilgrims and sojourners in this world. We Christians should be optimistic about the future because we know the One who holds the future.

Our Constitution still affords us many protections. Without a doubt, we enjoy the greatest amount of personal freedom of any nation on earth. We can still spread the Gospel without fear of imprisonment or death, although the right continues to be under attack. We can still choose to educate our children in Christian schools; however, those whose children remain in public schools must stay constantly on the alert to monitor what values they are being taught. We have not yet been forced to adopt an official state religion or non-religion, but our most basic religious freedoms are coming under increasing attack today from legislatures, courts, and anti-Christian legal groups.

The Tenth Amendment must be considered in understanding official state religions.

"The powers not delegated to the United States by the Constitution, nor prohibited by it to the States, are reserved to the States respectively, or to the people."

This is vital to understanding Jefferson's metaphor in the Danbury letter. Later generations have read the letter in terms of the language of their day and have assumed that Jefferson believed the First Amendment erected a wall of separation between all government and all religion. This is a misunderstanding based on the assumption that the generic term "State" alluded to all government.

The author himself said otherwise. Jefferson clearly believed that the wall of separation was not between all government and all religion, but rather between the national or federal government and religion, leaving the states free to be as religious as they wanted to be.

Whatever the separation of church and state means, it does not mean the separation of God from government.

The Key to Good Government

The key to good government is not how good our documents are or how good our laws are, but rather how good our leaders are. In America, whether or not the righteous rule depends totally upon the will of the voters—we have our choice.

In recent years, Christians have not taken their voting stewardship seriously. Of the more than 60 million evangelicals in America, as few as only 15 million vote. In fact, nearly half of evangelicals are not even registered.[13]

Although we did not ask to be born in America, we have been given our government as stewards, and we will be called upon to account for our stewardship at a later time. If our culture is moving the wrong

Thomas Jefferson

way, it is because of Christian non-involvement.

Former President James A. Garfield, a minister of the Gospel, once preached a revival during which 34 people came to Christ and were baptized. This type of activity is not usually associated with our presidents in the minds of most Americans. More than a century ago, Garfield reminded Americans:

President James A. Garfield

"Now, more than ever before, the people are responsible for the character of their Congress. If it be ignorant, reckless, and corrupt, it is because the people tolerate ignorance, recklessness, and corruption. If it be intelligent, brave, and pure, it is because the people demand these high qualities to represent them in the national legislature … [I]f the next centennial does not find us a great nation … it will be because those who represent the enterprise, the culture, and the morality of the nation do not aid in controlling the political forces."[14]

Those of us concerned with the culture and morality of the nation have done little to control its political forces, consequently our national policies do not now accurately reflect the values of the nation at large.

For example:

- 78 percent of the nation supports prayer in schools
- 74 percent want the Ten Commandments back in the classroom
- 68 percent want creation taught in the public schools
- 66 percent oppose partial birth abortions

Similarly high numbers join these in many other areas involving faith and values, yet our public policies do not reflect these high numbers. This is because Americans who embrace these values simply are not voting and not electing leaders who believe as they do.

Charles Finney

Reverend Charles Finney, a leader in America's second and third great awakenings during the early 1800s reminded Christians of a lesson we need to remember today:

"The Church must take right ground in regard to politics ... [The] time has come that Christians must vote for honest men and take consistent ground in politics ... Christians have been exceedingly guilty in this matter.... The time has come when they must act differently.... God cannot sustain this free and blessed country which we love and pray for unless the church will take right ground ... it seems sometimes as if the foundations of the nation are becoming rotten.... Christians seem to act as if they think God does not see what they do in politics. But I tell you, He does see it, and He will bless or curse this nation according to the course [Christians] take [in politics]."

It is time for Christians to reengage in civil stewardship from a biblical viewpoint in every arena of society and to influence society through voting and becoming involved in politics.

The U.S. Constitution forbids any religious test for public office, but it does not prohibit citizens from applying a religious test of their own in evaluating the candidates. If voters want a president who believes in God, then nothing in the constitution would prohibit them from lobbying those of like mind to work for such a candidate. Even with the ban on a religious test, every president since Washington (except Jefferson) has taken

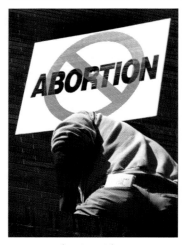

Abortion picketer

the oath of office with his hand on a Bible, promising to keep that oath by uttering "so help me, God."

Our forefathers have passed us the baton. We must now grip it with all our hearts, full of faith, rise up with a new conviction and a vision of who we are as God's children as we live in this "one nation under Him." We must have the courage to let our voice be heard, and we must rally our lives with a commitment to the real issues that matter to God and to this great nation. Then our lives will bear significance. It is a call that must cause us to be united. We must stand united, together with this conviction and say, "May God bless our nation." And let us gather around and inscribe for our motto:

Chief Justice Earl Warren

"Liberty and union, one and inseparable, now and forever. Christ first. Our country next."
—*President Andrew Jackson*

"I believe no one could read the history of our country without realizing the Good Book and the Spirit of the Savior have from the beginning been our guiding geniuses ... whether we look to the first Charter of Virginia, or to the Charter of New England, or to the Charter of Massachusetts Bay, or the Fundamental Orders of Connecticut, the same object is present; a Christian land governed by Christian principles ... I like to believe we are living today in the spirit of the Christian religion."
—*Chief Justice Earl Warren, February 15, 1954*

At the September 14, 2001 prayer service at National Cathedral, Reverend Billy Graham spoke for many when he said:

Rev. Billy Graham

"I have been asked hundreds of times in my life why God allows tragedy and suffering. I have to confess that I really do not know the answer totally, even to my own satisfaction. I have to accept by faith, that God is sovereign, and he is a God of love and mercy.

"Now we have a choice: whether to implode and disintegrate emotionally and spiritually as a people and a nation, or whether we choose to become stronger through all of this struggle to rebuild on a solid foundation. And I believe that we're in the process of starting to rebuild on that foundation. That foundation is our trust in God."

President John F. Kennedy

"I am proud of the revolutionary beliefs for which our forebears fought ... the belief that the rights of man come not from the generosity of the state but the hands of God."[15] —*President John F. Kennedy*

"Indeed, it is an indisputable fact that all the complex and horrendous questions confronting us at home and worldwide have their answer in [the Bible]."
—*President Ronald Reagan*

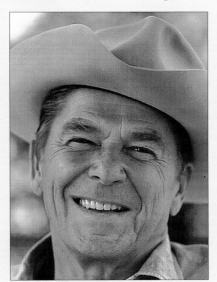

President Ronald Reagan

"You could not become thorough Americans if you think of yourselves in groups. America does not exist in groups. A man who thinks of himself as belonging to a particular nation in America has not yet become an American."
—*Woodrow Wilson, Address to New Citizens (1915)*

"The one absolutely certain way of bringing this nation to a ruin, of preventing all possibility of its continuing to be a nation at all, would be to permit it to become a tangle of squabbling nationalities."—*Theodore Roosevelt, Speech to the Knights of Columbus (1915)*

President Woodrow Wilson

Ronald Reagan once remarked, "We are told that God is dead. Well, He isn't. We just can't talk to Him in the classroom anymore."[16]

"History fails to record a single precedent in which nations subject to moral decay have not passed into political and economic decline. There has been either a spiritual awakening to overcome the moral lapse, or a progressive deterioration leading to ultimate national disaster."
—*General Douglas MacArthur*

President Theodore Roosevelt

"The choice before us is plain, Christ or chaos, conviction or compromise, discipline or disintegration. I am rather tired of hearing about our rights and privileges as American citizens. The time is come, it now is, when we ought to hear about the duties and responsibilities of our citizenship. America's future depends upon demonstrating God's government."
—*Peter Marshall, Senate Chaplain (1949)*

"This occasion is not alone the administration of the most sacred oath which can be assumed by an American citizen. It is a dedication and consecration under God to the highest office in service of our people. I assume this trust in the humility of knowledge that only through the guidance of Almighty Providence can I hope to discharge its ever-increasing burdens.... Knowing what the task means and the responsibility which it involves, I beg your tolerance, your aid, and your cooperation. I ask the help of Almighty God in this service to my country to which you have called me."
—*31st U.S. President, Herbert Clark Hoover, March 4, 1929, Inaugural Address*

President Herbert Hoover

"The world upheaval has added heavily to our tasks. But with the realization comes the surge of high resolve, and there is reassurance in belief in the God given destiny of our Republic. If I felt that there is to be sole responsibility in the Executive for the America of tomorrow I should shrink from the burden. But here are a hundred millions, with common concern and shared responsibility, answerable to God and country. The republic summons them to their duty, and I invite cooperation. I accept my part with single-mindedness of purpose and humility of spirit,

and implore the favor and guidance of God in His Heaven. With these I am unafraid, and confidently face the future. I have taken the solemn oath of office on that passage of Holy Writ herein it is asked: 'What doth the Lord require of thee but to do justly, and to love mercy, and to walk humbly with thy God.' This I plight to God and country."
—*29th U.S. President Warren G. Harding*
March 4, 1921, Inaugural Address

President Warren G. Harding

"As the family goes, so goes the nation and so goes the whole world in which we live."
—*Pope John Paul II (1920-2005)*

"I seek to encourage those Americans similarly inclined to help return America to its founding moral imperative. This is neither a cry for religious revolution nor a crusade; it is something else entirely. It is a reminder that we have lost our way. It is a suggestion that we return home again."
—*Rabbi Daniel Lapin*

"Christianity has not been tried and found wanting: It has been found difficult and not tried."
—*G. K. Chesterton (1874-1936)*

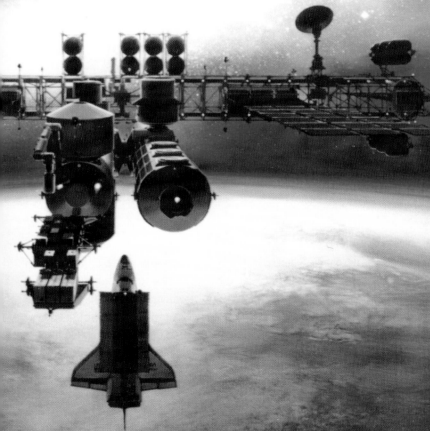

PART THREE
THE
FUTURE

✠

Chapter 10

The Battle for America

In April 1912, the largest and most luxurious vessel ever built set forth on its maiden voyage. The British liner Titanic had a double-bottomed hull, divided into sixteen watertight compartments. Because as many as four of these could be completely flooded without endangering the ship's buoyancy, the Titanic was considered unsinkable.

On the fateful night of April 14, shortly before midnight, the great liner was steaming through the foggy North Atlantic when it collided with an enormous iceberg. A 300-foot gash was ripped in the ship's right side, rupturing five of its watertight compartments. Even though it continued to send out S.O.S. signals to anyone who would listen, the Titanic sank into the icy depths, claiming more than 1500 lives.

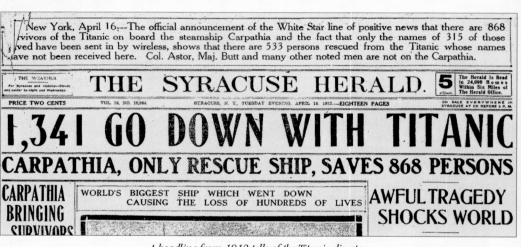

A headline from 1912 tells of the Titanic disaster

A tragic though often untold story about that night concerns one man on another ship, less than 20 miles away from the Titanic. The other vessel was the Californian, and it could have come to the rescue of the sinking vessel if only someone had been listening. Unfortunately for the passengers on the Titanic, the radio operator of the Californian had fallen asleep on duty! When help finally did arrive at the disaster area, it was too late for most of the passengers. The very greatness of the Titanic had caused her crew and passengers to feel inordinately confident. Unsinkable was such an assuring term, but it proved a fatal misjudgment.

Like the Titanic, our great ship of state, the United States of America, has gone adrift and is headed for a potentially fatal collision. Many feel she, too, is unsinkable; but that assessment is rooted in feeling, not fact. The truth of the matter is that America has already run into "icebergs" that have damaged her hull and caused more than a few leaks. She is in grave danger.

As our nation spirals downward, S.O.S. signals are being sent. Teenage delinquency, increased drug use, lower academic test scores, increased crime, spread of HIV-AIDS, pornography, Internet sex, homosexuality, and abortion are signals of a sinking society. Many, just like the sleeping radio operator, fail to hear the message. Fortunately, some are watching and listening. There are concerned friends who are alert to the danger. It is time for America to wake up and watch out! The message is clear: It is not too late ... yet.

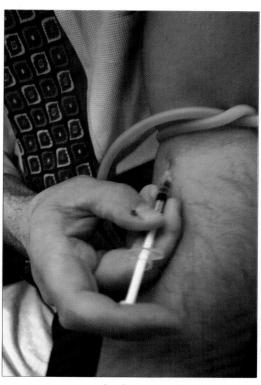

Drug use has become epidemic.

As we have seen, America was founded as a Christian nation. From Plymouth Rock to Independence Hall and beyond, the record is replete with evidence that ours is a nation deeply rooted in Christianity.[1] From the first Charter of Virginia, which spoke of "propagating of the Christian religion to such people, as yet live in darkness," to the U.S. Constitution, to federal proclamations of prayer and thanksgiving to God, to hundreds of our national monuments and thousands of legislative acts, letters, and personal papers of our original Founding Fathers, and federal proclamations of prayer and thanksgiving to God—all are abundant testimony to the claim that America was founded to be a biblical "city on a hill."

Although the U.S. Supreme Court concluded in 1892, "This is a Christian nation," much has changed since then. Our nation has drifted from the biblical moorings on which it was built. Americans have largely forgotten—or never learned—about the profound embedded role of biblical Christianity in America's rise from a colony of Britain to the mightiest nation on earth. Our current drift into moral relativism and cultural-wide amnesia toward our nation's religious heritage will continue for those who neglect or refuse to study our history.

America is out of control. It is a far cry from September 6, 1774 when the

Continental Congress opened with a reading of Psalm 35 and three hours of prayer before they commenced discussing the fate of the thirteen colonies that would become the United States of America. Based on the current attitude of secularists, most of our nation's founding documents would be considered unconstitutional today.

Christians should not apologize for believing in God or the trustworthiness of the Bible. The Bible calls on Christians to *defend* its truths with intensity and proficiency similar to the way a lawyer defends a client who is on trial for his life. Christians are *commanded* to defend the faith "always being ready to make a defense to every one who asks you to give an account for the hope that is in you, yet with gentleness and reverence. (I Peter 3:15)."

Numerous accounts in the Bible exemplify such defenses, arguments, and contentions, even though there was a high price to pay. The apostles defended the faith and were beaten and imprisoned for their efforts (Acts 4). Christians are instructed to "examine everything carefully" (I Thess. 5:21). John warns the Christian not to "believe every spirit" but to "test" them "to see whether they are from God." We are to examine everything—not just so-called "religious" issues.

The apologist's job, like a lawyer before a judge and jury, is to present sound arguments which testify to the truth. We should never say, "You be the judge." In a biblical defense of the Christian faith, God is not the one on trial. The Christian apologist does not have the option of taking a so-called neutral position when defending the faith. Even if a Christian wants to be neutral, he cannot, since neutrality is impossible. There's not much maneuvering room.

We cannot take a neutral position.

"A people without a heritage are easily persuaded." —*Karl Marx*

An apologetic methodology that claims a Christian should be open, objective, and tolerant of all opinions when the faith is defended is like a person who hopes to stop a man from committing suicide by taking the hundred-story plunge with the man in the hope he can convince the lost soul on the way down. A world without God and moral

absolutes leads to despair and moral anarchy. Once a person rejects Christianity, he has
not set himself free from the concept of faith
but instead has transferred it to something or
someone else. Jesus and His disciples were
constantly doing battle with opponents who
were considerably meaner than today's antag-
onists. Jesus was not passive in the face of
hostility and opposition toward Him. He met
His attackers head-on and systematically
demolished their arguments.[2]

The Bible is the standard of truth. It
presents a specific view of the world, man,
God, and authority. Anything that is not
consistent with the biblical worldview is not
true. The Bible is also the Christian's ethical
standard. It teaches us to distinguish between
right and wrong. The commandments
contained therein are from God and present
us with our ethical duty.

The Bible is our standard of truth.

"A new worldview is emerging which
calls into question all traditional notions of truth, structure, and reality. It is
called postmodernism. This philosophy removes the anchor of objective truth
and pushes human experience into the chaotic sea of human preference and
subjectivity. Postmodernism says that while absolute truth was once a viable
belief, it has turned out to be little more than a passing fad."[3]

Christian Responsibility

Our society, conditioned to think in terms of moral and ethical relativism, needs the
input of people of faith who recognize absolute principles. A thought system, based on
faith and an upward evolutionary process combined with unlimited human potential,
needs to challenge those who do not hold a biblical view of God. Secular humanists have
not stolen America—Christians have given it to them!

Christians are guilty of retreating from public life and neglecting their responsibility
to be "salt and light" to the world. This has created a vacuum in our society. We have a
"ghetto mentality" in which we read our own literature, listen to our own music, stay out
of politics, and let the rest of the world go by.[4] This mentality has given opportunity for
secular-minded individuals to take over influential posts in academia, government, politics, and the media where they can easily promote humanistic goals.

People of faith have a vital contribution to make to the well-being of America. They are needed to articulate biblical principles of government. In every courtroom, legislative hall, and school in the nation, we must articulate these principles.

We need to reestablish the moral tone of society. Our Founding Fathers recognized that freedom cannot exist in an immoral society—the nation will crumble from within or be conquered from without.

History shows that those who founded the United States consciously intended America to be a Christian nation, guided above all else by the truths of the Bible. The fundamental principles for the laws and liberties of this new nation were found in the Ten Commandments of the Old Testament and the Sermon on the Mount of the New Testament.

Revisionist historians have tried to blur the facts of history, but the documented evidence of our origins is too powerful to suppress. It was a Christian America that opened

Ellis Island welcomed immigrants to America.

its arms to the world and guaranteed what we now pledge as "liberty and justice for all." It was the spiritual, oral, and ethical teaching of Christianity that brought about our unparalleled prosperity as a nation.[5]

There are six great spheres in which every Christian should be vitally interested and involved:

- **The world**
- **Humanity**
- **Our nation**
- **Our schools**
- **Our churches**
- **The family**

Every church and synagogue should be endeavoring to do what it can to strengthen each of these great spheres.[6]

Christians on many sides are openly defamed, deployed, mocked, and marginalized. Clearly, calmly, and boldly, we should stop apologizing, hiding, and pretending we can coexist peacefully with the perverse new faith that has seized control of North American culture.

Chuck Colson

"We've been fighting cultural skirmishes on all sides without knowing what the war is about. We have not identified the worldviews that lie at the root of cultural conflict. The culture war is not just about abortion, homosexual rights, or the decline of public education. These are only skirmishes. The real war is a cosmic struggle between world views—between the Christian worldview and the various secular and spiritual worldviews arrayed against it. This is what we must understand if we are going to be effective in evangelizing our world today and in transforming it to reflect the wisdom of the Creator."[7]
—*Charles Colson*

We are engaged in a struggle between traditional values and moral relativism, between morality and humanism. Today there is a twisted concept of tolerance—not simply the recognition that everyone is entitled to believe as they wish, but the insistence that no set of values is better or worse than any others. Stretching intolerance into moral blindness produces devastating outcomes for our society.

The Tyranny of Tolerance[8]

They are the people who won't wish you a Merry Christmas; who think infants in the womb are almost like fecal matter; who never met a criminal who couldn't be rehabilitated; who think Hollywood is a better moral compass than the Vatican; who think men and women are identical, except when it comes to a man making even mildly suggestive remarks to a woman; who deny the individual right to keep and bear arms (and who don't think much of the military, either); who think perverted sexual conduct is a constitutional right; who think racial quotas are salutary as long as they operate against whites and Asians; who think that public schools benefit from no discipline and no competition; and, above all, who think that God should be expunged from the public square.

If we truly believe that promiscuity, infidelity, homosexuality, and drug abuse are related to areas of decline of American life, why in the world are we not saying something about it?

If conservatives want to change the culture, we have to begin by speaking up for our own point of view. If the highest price we pay for our beliefs is a few snickers from our opponents, then we should consider ourselves most fortunate.

The Remaking of America[9]

America's Christian heritage is a fading memory for most Americans. Decades of value-neutral public education have left our nation without a moral anchor. While the Bible is a perennial bestseller, and Americans purchase more Bibles than any other people on earth, "the Bible has virtually disappeared from American education. It is rarely studied, even as literature, in public classrooms."[10] How is it that a nation that seems to be in love with the Bible works so hard to reject its teachings? While Americans seem to honor the Bible, they are ignorant of its contents. "Americans revere the Bible but by and large they don't read it. And because they don't read it, they have become a nation of biblical illiterates."[11] Six out of ten Americans have no idea who delivered the Sermon on the Mount, and fewer than half of those surveyed can name the four gospels.

The Bible can change America's future.

America is being defined in terms of "multiculturalism." An appreciation of diverse cultures is being used as a cover-up to smuggle in aberrational moral standards that have the effect of diluting the impact of biblical Christianity.[12]

> "Polytheism [all gods are equal] leads to relativism [all moral codes are equal]; relativism leads to humanism [man makes his own laws]; and humanism leads to statism [the state best represents mankind as the pinnacle of power]. As Rushdoony remarks, 'Because an absolute law is denied, it means that the only universal law possible is an imperialistic law, a law imposed by force and having no validity other than the coercive imposition.'"[13]

Multiculturalists want to make a name for themselves by displacing the name of God and forcing the position that all cultures are inherently equal. Our children are being cheated out of a factual and true history sacrificed on the altar of political correctness.

"We have defended the right to engage in polygamy. We defend the freedom of choice for mature, consenting individuals."[14] —*Nadine Strossen, ACLU President, at Yale Law School (2005)*

"I can't see that there's any rational justification for prohibiting [polygamy]. As long as it's between consenting adults, it ought to be permitted."[15] —*Michele Parish Pixler, Former Executive Director ACLU of Utah (1990)*

"When the state forces parents to be involved [in their children's lives], the consequences are catastrophic."[16] —*Howard Simon, ACLU of Florida (2003)*

At 8:45 a.m. EST on September 11, 2001, a grim reality appeared suddenly on the American horizon. The world watched in shock and disbelief as three thousand men and

A cross made from the girders of the WTC

women died in the deadliest assault to hit these shores in nearly four hundred years of history. It was a sobering moment for every American as we considered the carnage, the prospect that this unprovoked attack was but a prelude to something worse, and the even more disquieting feeling that something awful was about to happen and we were powerless to stop it. It was the fear that, in one terrible moment of unspeakable horror, the world had changed forever. The attack by Middle Eastern terrorists and the devastating collapse of the World Trade Center towers are emblematic of the world in which we live. Catastrophe had come when we least expected it. It would take months to sort it all out as America wept.

America's doors are open for people of all faiths—or no faith—to live here and practice their religion unmolested. But that's not despite our Christian heritage—it is an outgrowth of it! Millions upon millions of people around the world would love to live in America because of our freedoms. Muslims and other non-Christians arrived as guests in this country, and now are citizens. Yet, no one has the right to declare that I must convert to another religion or be killed as is the commonplace circumstance in many Islamic countries. Our media, however, seems to see little difference between Islam and evangelical Christianity.[17] Mohammed commanded Muslims to fight against all infidels if they do not embrace Islam, as well as against the people of the Book (the Scriptures), that is, Jews and Christians. The Hadith speaks of conversion to Islam by compulsion.

Twin Memorial lights at the World Trade Center site

Mohammed said, "I have been ordered to fight against the people until they testify that none has the right to be worshiped but Allah, that Mohammed is Allah's prophet, and they offer prayers and give obligatory charity. If they perform all of that, they save their lives and their property" (Sahih Bukhari, Vol. 1, Bk 2, No. 24). Mohammed said, "Whosoever has killed an enemy and has proof of that will possess his spoils" (Sahih Bukhari, Vol. 4, Bk 53, No. 370).[18]

There is an infinite gulf between these teachings and the teachings of Jesus that declare, "You shall love your neighbor as yourself." Jesus said, "Love your enemies" (Matt. 5:44).

Islam is a religion that has no real evidence to support it, whereas Christianity has the evidence of Jesus Christ—His miracles, His perfect life, and most importantly, the evidence of His resurrection from the dead. The fact, for instance, that Jesus lived on earth, was given an unfair trial, was put to death by crucifixion, and was raised from the dead is undeniable and recognized by nearly all religious faiths. Even historians have told us we have incredible evidence of Christ's resurrection— more so than we have of any event in ancient history. Dr. Thomas Arnold, 19th century professor of history at Oxford University and author of *History of Rome*, wrote:

"I have been used for many years to study the histories of other times, and to examine and weigh the evidence of those who have written about them, and I know of no one fact in the history of mankind which is proved by better and fuller experience of every sort, to the understanding of a fair inquirer, than the great sign which God hath given us that Christ died and rose again from the dead."[19]

Time for a Spiritual Rebirth

Dr. Thomas Arnold

"Men have forgotten God."— *Alexander Solzhenitsyn (1918 - ...)*

In today's culture war, strict separationists battle tirelessly to scrub out any mention of God from all public life and documents. Yet legions of Christians living in America have resigned for a multitude of reasons from the conflict which rages in our land. Many admit we are irreversibly marching toward Armageddon and say we should simply concentrate on saving souls as we withdraw from an increasingly corrupt world. In reality, we are called upon to be soldiers of Christ, equipped with the full armor of God. It's not the sound of action that is deafening, it's the sound of silence.

Ours, apparently, is a land that has abandoned its own heritage. Are we prepared

today to give up the comforts, material wealth, and perhaps our very lives to help spark a spiritual rebirth in this nation? This experiment, unprecedented in history, that our Founding Fathers began based on biblical principles for the glory of God, has now come full term.

Radical secularists intend to remove from government property virtually every tincture of Christian content and influence. The scope of the attack on the Christian faith is breathtaking. By our inaction, we have given strength to those who oppose us.

Secularism takes many forms. It morphs to mask its real identity. "Secularism is . . . the result of a vacuum of God-centered Christianity in the culture," writes Michael Horton in *Beyond Culture Wars*. "Having trusted too much in the idols of nation, pragmatism, ideology, and secular power, whether the carved image is in the shape of a donkey or an elephant, the stage is perhaps set for a return to the main message and mission of the church."[20] "In the culture wars, the Gospel has been a casualty—not from the shells of the secularist but from the 'friendly fire' of its own soldiers."[21]

Erwin Lutzer, pastor of Moody Memorial Church in Chicago asks, "Will America be given another chance?" He answers, "Whether America has another chance is up to God; whether we are faithful is up to us."[22] Revived Christians beget revival. "It must begin with us, in our own homes where our true character is revealed, and in our churches where our burning hearts can ignite others."

We may glibly proclaim that we want this nation to have another chance to capture the meaning of In God We Trust. But if we knew what such a transformation would personally demand, we might just prefer to leave things as they are. Many of us may have become too comfortable to pay the price. Have you?

Are we prepared to recapture the self-discipline of our forefathers which made this nation great? We do not need a political revolution—we need a spiritual revival. Our founders pledged their lives, fortunes, and sacred honor to exercise their civic duty. What are 21st century Christians willing to pledge?

Our nation has met many struggles and trials with amazing success, but we have always turned to God to get us through. Now is the time for the heroes to return to moral sanity. Now is the time for the men and women who trust in the one true God to:

We must humble ourselves and pray.

- Humble themselves before God,
- Promise to live according to a higher standard of righteousness, and
- Be willing to sacrifice themselves to fulfill our nation's true calling.

Patrick Henry said:

"They tell us we are weak, unable to cope with so formidable an adversary. But when shall we be stronger? Will it be next week or next year? If we make proper use of the means which God of nature has placed in our power, we shall not fight our battle alone. There is a just God who presides over the destinies of nations and who will raise up friends to fight our battles for us."[23]

Now is the time to place our feet firmly on the stepping stones of our forefathers so that we, in turn, will provide other stones for the great work of advancing the faith of those who follow.

We have been infected with the spirit of fear. We must not be afraid of the culture or afraid of sinners. We tend to embrace a false definition of holiness—one that makes it acceptable to isolate ourselves from people Jesus wants us to reach. Do not run from evil or retreat from unbelievers at the same time.

Some believers today have taken separation from the world to an extreme. They mistake sanitized isolation for holiness. Jesus, on the other hand, was willing to go anywhere to talk with anyone, because He was more concerned with His mission than He was with His image. He wasn't afraid of thieves, nor mortified by the sight of prostitutes. He engaged the culture without fear.[24]

We should not be hardened with anger because current American culture may not accept or welcome our influence. Today is a time for influence—not just for huffing and puffing in attempting to reclaim our lost laws, but with persuasion and perseverance in addressing the horror of abortion, the collapse of heterosexual marriage, and taking God out of education.

We should not allow ourselves to become brainwashed into believing that because we live in a multicultural society, we cannot make judgments in a culture which grows sicker and more corrupt by the minute.

- The traditional family unit is being attacked on every side.

- Higher and higher taxes

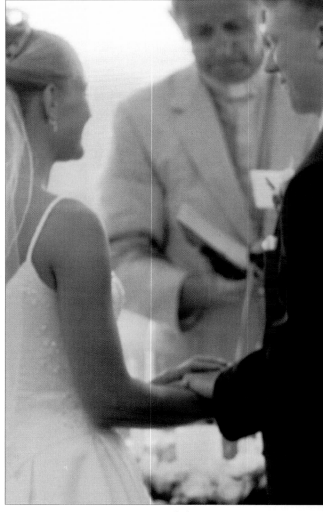

Marriage is a holy institution.

continue to burden a smaller and smaller group of hard-working citizens.

- Our public schools have become a conduit for anti-family, anti-religion, and anti-morality messages.

- The entertainment industry pours immorality and violence into the minds of our children on a daily basis.

We must strengthen the traditional family.

The list could go on and on. Television, film, music, art, politics, the justice system, higher education, and the news media are used by the elite left to proclaim their constant special-interest-group rhetoric.

The concept of America as a Christian nation has been systematically blotted from the collective memory of this country. It sounds like an alien philosophy, an intrusion of religion into a secular nation.

Patrick Henry, Christian patriot and the golden-tongued orator of the Revolutionary period, wrote in his will:

"I have not disposed of all my property to my family. There is one more thing that I wish I could give them. That is the Christian religion. If they had that and I had not given them one shilling, they would have been rich; and if they had not that and I had given them the world, they would be poor." [25]

The Judeo-Christian heritage that made this nation great in the first place has been sifting through our fingers like sand because too many Christians are "engaged simply in personal peace and prosperity." The question then is, "How do we reclaim America?" The cultural mandate (Gen. 1:28) directs us to "be fruitful, and multiply, and replenish the earth," and have dominion over "all" things. The last commandment (the Great Commission) is to spread His Word unto all the world (Matt. 28:18-20).

The solution, according to Reverend Peter Marshall, is:
1. Go deeper in Jesus personally, as individuals. This is the centerpiece of the New Testament and the centerpiece of everything.
2. Build deeper relationships with each other. You cannot grow in the Christian life beyond a certain point all by yourself.

3. Get more deeply involved in the society around us as "salt and light." Mission, outreach, and ministry flow out of the shared life in Jesus Christ. It's not created by committee and not the function of programs—it's a function of that shared life in Jesus.

These are the three stages of revival, and one leads to the other. Gary Bauer, one-time presidential candidate and former president of Family Research Council, was interviewed by Dan Rather who inquired, "What do you want for America?"
Gary responded:

Gary Bauer

"I want to see an America ... where I don't have to worry about date rape when my daughter goes out for the first time at college. I want an America where, when a young man pledges to love and cherish and honor her for the rest of their lives, there's a good chance he means it. I want a country where children come first again and where virtue is honored; a place where values matter and the American dream is still real. I want a country where families no longer have to hide behind barred windows, where criminals do real

time and aren't released on a whim or a technicality. I want a place where children can play in public parks again without fear, and where adults can walk across those parks at night."[26]

What Bauer was asking for is quite reasonable. There are cities in this world with huge populations—in the Orient, Europe, and Africa—where you can go for a late evening walk around the public park with no fear for your life. It was once like that here in America, but sadly, this is no longer the case.

Bauer continued:

"Families would spend more time being real families, not watching artificial ones on television. I hope for a land where love of country is seen as a virtue again. Where the young are taught the unique blessing they have received just to have been born in such a place.

We need to spend quality time with our family.

"In my America, the schools would work once more. Political correctness would be thrown out, and the goal of education would once again be to teach our children to have 'knowing heads and loving hearts.'

"In this land, racism, and special rights, would be rejected, and all our children would be taught to judge their fellow citizens by the content of their character, not the color of their skin. I see a country that respects life again, where drive-by shootings and one and a half million aborted babies each year are seen as disasters. Here responsibilities would be as important as rights, and a handshake would be something (once again) to rely on. In my country, working men and women would be praised, not penalized by ever-growing government. The truly poor would get a hand up, not a hand out."

Our culture has gone from the strong family values of a society with a Christian consensus to a society that glorifies violence, illicit sex, and rebellion. We have severed ourselves from the roots of what made us great in the first place. We have gone from *Leave It to Beaver* to *Beavis and Butthead* in forty years.[27]

The Gospel must go forth unhindered and uncensored.

All nations that have ever existed were founded upon some theistic or anti-theistic principle, whether Hinduism of India, Confucianism of China, Mohammedanism of Saudi Arabia, or atheism of modern China and the former Soviet Union. Today, many in the U.S. are busily working to tear apart our rich Christian foundation that made us great. In no way am I advocating theocracy, but I do advocate a return, as much as possible, to the faith of our nation's Founders—a full religious liberty once again so the Gospel can go forth unhindered and uncensored. We should call for an end to the secular witch hunt against "any sneaky vestiges of religion left in public places." It is time to stop the state-sanctioned atheism that has been stripping the public square of plaques of the Ten Commandments or anything else that offends secular sensibilities.

God's Actions in America

In the 1960s, historian Helmut Thielecke wrote:

"When the drama of history is over, Jesus Christ will stand alone upon the stage. All the great figures of history—Pharoah, Alexander the Great, Charlemagne, Churchill, Stalin ... Mao Tse-Tung—will realize they have been but actors in a drama produced by another."

Governments exist by the authority of Almighty God.

Like George Washington, God established this land of America as a nation in His providence, a nation unique in the history of the world. America is the first nation in the history of this planet that was established on the basis of freedom of religion. Sadly, many today have never been taught this truth.

God set our continent apart—separating it from others by two oceans—not to be discovered until around the time of the Reformation. God established a unique nation, founded by the Pilgrims, Puritans, and others who arrived here possessing evangelical Christianity. The Bible was believed and the Gospel preached. It was an evangelical nation. As late as 1775, 98 percent of the people were of Christian persuasion.[28] It is tragic that we as Christians have failed to maintain constant vigil over our religious freedoms. The withdrawal of faith-based citizens from the public arena has emboldened others to declare that our values are no longer welcome. Now we face a tough fight to change the direction of our nation.

The ACLU, Americans United for Separation of Church and State, and Freedom from Religion, Inc. have attempted to create an environment wherein government and religion are adversaries, intoning the mantra of "separation of church and state."[29]

Have you ever noticed how some of the most intolerant men and women are those who clamor the loudest for tolerance? Their view of free speech is that you can have complete free-speech rights if you agree with their views and toe their line. Woe to you if you dare say, for example, that homosexuality is wrong. Today's version of so-called "tolerance" in reality is anything but broad-minded.

It is time for us to discern once again between good and evil. Dr. Paul Vitz, professor at New York University, observes that the moral decline in America is directly related to the widespread acceptance of this myth:

"One of the major characteristics of moral decline in the United States in recent decades has been the rapid growth of moral relativism. The idea is now widespread that each individual has some kind of sovereign right to create, develop, and express whatever values he or she happens to prefer."[30]

Sometimes the most intolerant scream the loudest.

Surely, this echoes what the Bible says about ancient Israel during the time of the judges: "Everyone did what was right in his own eyes" (Judges 12:25). What the Bible said more than three thousand years ago is just as true today as it was then.[31]

However, this tolerance really means an intolerance of the absolutes of Christianity. This false idea of tolerance has subtly undermined Christianity, and most Christians have not recognized what really has been happening. Many Christians have been deceived into believing they have no right to impose their view on society.[32]

At one time, a group called "Toleration" began. They were insisting on a tolerance of all religious ways, beliefs, and customs.... And most of the things of which they were intolerant were related to Christianity. What they really meant was that they wanted a tolerance of anything in society, except Christianity!

The idea of open-mindedness comes from the notion that there is no such thing as absolute truth, or that truth cannot be absolutely known. Some say, 'There are no absolutes.' Ironically, this premise has become their one absolute. Such ideas are derived from an anti-biblical philosophy which holds that everything is relative.

There has been a fundamental shift. Our society is now based on a relative morality: that is, a person can do what he likes and is answerable to no one but himself as long as the majority of people can be persuaded that their interests are not being threatened. This results in society's being told that no one can say anything against those who choose to be sexual deviants, go naked publicly, or do whatever they want (within the limits of the law, which is also changing to become more "tolerant" of people's actions).[33]

The idea that you can do whatever you want is rampant.

Discrimination against Christians in American society is common. While tolerance is touted as the highest virtue in our popular culture, Christians are often subjected to scorn and ridicule and even denied their religious freedoms. Anti-Christian discrimination occurs in a variety of contexts throughout our culture, from the public to the private sectors, and in mainstream media and Hollywood. The discrimination is becoming more blatant and widespread each day. The cultural assumptions of our society influence changes in the law, and the culture is moving against the public expression of Christian belief.

The purpose of the Establishment Clause was to prevent the federal government from establishing a national denomination, which would serve to inhibit our religious freedoms. It was never intended to keep Christianity out of the public square. Today, the Establishment Clause is routinely used to suppress people's free exercise rights of religion in our schools and public life.[34] The original Establishment Clause restricted the federal government, not the states. Its language, "Congress shall make no law ..." makes it clear the federal government was precluded from establishing a national religion and precluded from interfering with the rights of individual states to do as they pleased respecting the establishment of their own religions.

Later, the Fourteenth Amendment was ratified, and the Supreme Court, in a series of decisions, ruled the First Amendment Establishment Clause was applicable to the states through incorporation in the Due Process Clause of the Fourteenth Amendment.

When the Constitution was written, Christian religious instruction was the primary purpose of education.[35] For most people, the rising wall of separation did not become apparent until the Supreme Court outlawed state-sponsored prayer in public schools in *Engel v. Vitale*[36] in 1962.

Some say that Engel did not take God out of the schools but merely prohibited state-sponsored prayer. Unfortunately, this analysis is oversimplified. It does not take much state activity at all to trigger state sponsorship under modern case law. *Wallace v. Jaffree*[37] held that public schools may not even set aside a period of silence at the commencement of the school day if there is a mere suggestion that students might use the time for prayer. It strains the imagination to conceive how moments of silence constitute state endorsement of religion, especially a particular religion. The law, nonetheless, seems to be what the Supreme Court says it is.

Defending Our Flag

What do you feel when you see our flag waving majestically? I think of the men and women who gave their lives protecting our flag and the freedoms for which it stands. I see a symbol of our national unity.

Throughout our history, the flag has inspired defenders of our freedoms to press on to the goal, to achieve great deeds when nothing less would suffice. The mere sight of Old Glory waving majestically reminded them of America—a home and a flag worth defending.

In 1989, the Supreme Court, in response to a flag-burning Communist, amended the Constitution by inserting flag-burning into the Bill of Rights. Their decision took

away a fundamental right of the American people, a right we possessed since our birth as a nation—the right to protect our flag.

Take a look at what the courts have done with pornography, prayer, the Ten Commandments, the Pledge of Allegiance, and marriage. Our courts are wrong when they tell us prayer can't be protected under free speech but pornography can. They are wrong when they do not allow the Bible or the Ten Commandments in our schools.

The American values we share are a legacy, and we should desire to preserve them so they can be passed on to our children and grandchildren. American values have their basis in the Declaration of Independence and Constitution. The flag of the United States symbolizes these values. Flag desecration is not speech, and it desecrates our Constitution to say so.

Helping Our Children Become Leaders

Our mandate is to help children from a very young age not merely to be Christians, but to be potent Christians. When they walk into the room, they should be the ones who shape the conversation, being the salt and light that Jesus talked about. It isn't just for extraverts. It is a mandate, and if teens learn to be ashamed of their faith (because of their parents' lifestyles), then they will think it rather strange we want their friends to come to Christ.

Let them know they were born for greatness! They are here to make an impact. God brought them into the world because He has something special that only they can do. There is a greatness inside them.

In the minds of our children, it should not be "if" God wants to use them but "how" God wants to use them. They may not know how to start, and that is where you will be of great help. Don't pour cold water on their passionate idealistic notions of how they can change their school or change their world. Help them think through what it would take, in practical terms, to accomplish such feats. As your children come to you with their ideas, you will be joining the ranks of other parents throughout history whose children have changed the world!

"The pop techno-terrorists are slowly sucking the life out of the whole generation. They mesmerize teens into a state of apathy and program them to exist in a world that makes the media-shapers even wealthier. They steal youthful dreams and potential.

The next generation of leaders

They use free speech as an exercise to market whatever appeals to the lower nature. Then, once they make their millions, we honor them as entrepreneurial geniuses and role models."[38]

Principals, teachers, and school boards (due to misunderstanding and misinterpretation) have assisted in the denial of the Constitutional rights of students and teachers. The world is watching to see if we will be motivated to impact our culture, to deal with the moral crises in our society, and to reclaim our families and children.[39]

Christians should look at secular higher education and ask, "Do we really want the best and brightest born-again young people educated in the philosophy that dominates American academia? Do we want our young leaders to become Christian humanists or Christian leaders?"

Christian parents of potential leaders need to wake up to reality. The Barna Group research found that very few teenagers today make decisions based on moral or spiritual values. They base their decisions on whatever feels right or comfortable to them at the time, making them easy targets for left-wing professors. Students need help in standing strong in the face of the immoral and political onslaughts they receive at college.

Good parenting starts early.

Church attendance drops off dramatically between the ages 18 and 29. Secular college education systematically denigrates Christian values. The themes and viewpoints dominating the world view of these secular colleges are:

• Diversity is the god of modern education. It worships all lifestyles and generally treats conservative Christianity with disdain. Conservatives on American campuses are often pronounced as being intellectually inferior and irreversibly bigots.

• The knowledge of God and belief in His gifts of an unchanging code of moral ethics is ridiculed as belonging to the unenlightened.

• Perverse forms of sexual behavior are not only considered acceptable but celebrated. Campuses boast prominently open homosexual professors.

• America was and is the number one terrorist state. Criticism for our nation's history and an attitude of dissent brings an unbelievable level of anti-Americanism.[40]

The present public education system is actually one of the main reasons for the majority of our problems—it is not God's method of training future generations, but it is the world's (or man's) method and needs to be changed. The following are some ideas that can help change the education of our children in positive ways:

- Parents should assume the role of overseeing the education of their children. They must be involved, whether they send their children to public school, Christian schools, or home school them.
- Churches should provide suport for homeschooling parents and supplement the public education with Christian perspectives and history.
- Businesses should participate through apprenticeship programs.

It's important to get involved in your child's education.

- Each of us should work to bring back a Christian philosophy and methodology to education in America.
- New Christian colleges should be started and current ones can be encouraged.

Whoever controls the education of our children controls the future of our nation. The way in which teachers execute their responsibility of training those that have been entrusted to their care will determine the future course of America. Leaders in the field of education admit there are problems with the existing education system. Ironically, most of them suggest increased funding or more centralizing of education. A lack of money is not really the problem—look at the facts:[41]

- In 1950, $8.8 billion was spent on education in America.
- Thirty-five years later, in 1985, $261 billion was spent on education.
- In 1990, $353 billion was paid out.
- In 1992, $445 billion was consumed on education.
- On average, well over $5,000 is spent per student, per year, on secondary public education.

- In 2008, the amount spent on education was nearly 600 billion.[42]

Although much money has been spent on our schools, our courts have consistently undermined any Christian influences there.

- Verbal prayer offered in a school is unconstitutional, even if voluntary and denominationally neutral.
- If a student prays over his lunch, it is unconstitutional for him to pray out loud.
- Students are prohibited from reading Bibles silently during free time or even to open their Bibles at school.
- It is unconstitutional for a classroom library to contain books that deal with Christianity or for a teacher to be seen with a personal copy of the Bible at school.
- Students cannot bring Christmas cookies with the colors of red and green or in the shapes of stars or bells.

From the administration to the student government, from the professorate to the student media, college students cannot escape the clutches of rabid liberalism.[43] Liberals dominate the university scene. This shouldn't come as much of a surprise, but the extent of their domination is mind-boggling. The brainwashing of students by the university

system is one of the most severe problems plaguing America's youth. Under higher education's façade of objectivity lies a grave and overpowering bias against Christians, a bias that deeply affects the student body. Lack of financial resources is not the problem in our public schools. The problem is a lack of spiritual resources.

There are two basic ways of thinking in life—one that is according to the world and one that is according to Christ. The worldly, or humanistic, way of thinking is "man-centered," and it always brings captivity or bondage. On the other hand, the Christian way of thinking always brings liberty. For the past several decades, a worldly philosophy has dominated our educational system. God has been expelled from public school. Prayer was removed in 1962, Bible reading in 1963, and the Ten Commandments in 1980 and 2006.

Verbal prayer in school is unconstitutional.

If we really care about the world our children will inherit, something must be done. The crisis in higher education is not only the risk of indoctrination through the vagaries of pluralism, tolerance, and diversity, but also the fact that "value-neutral" socialization and radical sexual indoctrination are robbing many young Americans of their future, their competitiveness, and their cultural inheritance.

How many parents, preparing to send their children off to some prestigious institution, have considered the possibility that the four-year indoctrination program, for which they will spend possibly a hundred thousand dollars or more, will yield a product they no longer recognize as their own offspring? How many parents will appreciate the indoctrination and demoralization that will be forced upon their children?

The source of the problem, as author David Horowitz has said many times, is a lack of accountability among university faculty and administrators to the people who pay their salaries. Furthermore, it is a sign of utter contempt for those who will ultimately employ the graduates of these institutions. University chancellors, trustees, presidents, deans, and faculty members have become accustomed to using their endowments and the funds provided by donors, foundations, tuition monies, and other industry and federal grants, to do as they please.[44]

It falls to people like you and me—parents, students, and others who truly care—to take matters into our own hands and band with a growing coalition of like-minded groups who are ready to lend a hand. The most conspicuous victories for free speech and equal access in recent years have come from legal challenges, including litigation through the full range of judicial options, by groups such as the Center for Individual rights (CIR), the Alliance Defense Fund (ADF), and the Foundation for Individual Rights in Education (FIRE). These non-profit organizations, all privately funded and passionate about their mission, are having a profound impact on campus debates by providing an escape valve for students and faculty

What will your child face when he or she starts school?

who find themselves caught in the web of the censorship and viewpoint discrimination.[45]

- Verbal prayer offered in a school is unconstitutional, even if it is both denominationally neutral and participation is voluntary. *Engel v. Vitale, 1962; Abington v. Schempp, 1963; Commissioner of Education v. School committee of Leyden, 1971.*
- Freedom of speech is guaranteed to students who speak at school assemblies where attendance is voluntary unless that speech includes a prayer. *Stein v. Oshinsky, 1965; Collins v. Chandler Unified School District, 1981.*
- If a student prays over lunch, it is unconstitutional for him to pray aloud. *Reed v. van Hoven, 1965.*
- It is unconstitutional for kindergarten students to recite: "We thank you for the birds that sing; We thank you [God] for everything," even though the word "God" is not uttered. *DeSpain v. DeKalb County Community School District, 1967.*
- It is unconstitutional to set up a Nativity scene in the lobby of a county government building. *County of Allegheny v. American Civil Liberties Union Greater Pittsburgh Chapter, 1989.*
- It is unconstitutional for a war memorial to be erected in the shape of a cross. *Lowe v. City of Eugene, 1969.*
- It is unconstitutional for students to arrive at school early to hear a student volunteer read prayers. *State Board of Education v. Board of Education of Netcong, 1970.*
- It is unconstitutional for a Board of Education to "reference" God or "biblical instruction" in any of its official writings related to standards for operation of schools. *State v. Whisner, 1976.*
- It is unconstitutional for a classroom library to contain books that deal with

Christianity or for a teacher to be seen with a personal copy of the Bible at school. *Roberts v. Madigan, 1990.*

- It is unconstitutional for a public cemetery to have a planter in the shape of a cross because it might cause "emotional distress" and constitute an "injury-in-fact." *Warsaw v. Tehachapi, 1990.*
- It is unconstitutional for the Ten Commandments to hang on the walls of a classroom even if they are purchased by private funds. *Stone v. Graham, 1980; Ring v. Grand Forks Public School District, 1980; Lanner v. Wimmer, 1981.*
- A bill becomes unconstitutional even though the wording may be constitutionally acceptable, if the legislator who introduced the bill had a religious purpose in his mind when he authored it. *Wallace v. Jaffree, 1985.*
- It is unconstitutional for a kindergarten class to recite: "God is great; God is good, let us thank Him for our food." *Wallace v. Jaffree, 1984.*
- It is unconstitutional for a graduation ceremony to contain an opening or a closing prayer. *Graham v. Central Community School District, 1985; Disselbrett v. Douglas School District. 1986.*
- In the city seal, it is unconstitutional for any symbol to depict religious heritage or any religious element of the community. *Robinson v. City of Edmond, 1995; Harris v. City of Zion, 1991; Kuhn v. City of Rolling Meadows, 1991; Friedman v. Board of County Commissioners, 1985.*
- It is unconstitutional for a kindergarten class to ask during a school assembly whose birthday is celebrated on Christmas. *Florey v. Sioux Falls School District, 1979.*

In Pennsylvania, because a prosecuting attorney mentioned seven words from the Bible in the courtroom, a jury sentence was overturned for a man convicted of brutally clubbing a seventy-one-year-old woman to death.

What Is the Solution?

To turn America from being a nation at risk to being a nation on the rise, we need a new generation of well-trained and educated youth who are knowledgeable of the truth and know how to think biblically.

- Encourage your children and others to familiarize themselves with the Declaration of Independence, the Constitution, and the Federalist Papers (authored by James Madison, John Jay, and Alexander Hamilton), which expound on the Founders' original intent for each branch of government.
- Aggressively resist the efforts of philosophical minorities who are destroying our educational process. We have backed off too long into complacency and non-involvement about our nation's schools.

- Teach your children about the hundreds of examples of God being mentioned in our laws and monuments.
- Teach your children to be discerning of the discrimination in our schools, media, and government towards Christianity.
- Ignore newly updated and revised American history school textbooks that have largely erased Christianity from our colonial history.

Abraham Lincoln asserted schools are the future:

"The philosophy of the school room in one generation will be the philosophy of the government in the next."

Noah Webster perceptively described the importance of a good educational system:

"Education of youth should be watched with the most scrupulous attention. Education ... forms the moral characters of men, and morals are the basis of government. Education should therefore be the first care of ... political regulations; for it is much easier to introduce and establish an effectual system for preserving morals, than to correct by penal statutes the ill effects of a bad system...."[46]

President James Garfield, in an address celebrating the Declaration of Independence, stated:

"Now, more than ever, the people are responsible for the character of their Congress. If that body be ignorant, reckless, and corrupt, it is because the people tolerate ignorance, recklessness, and corruption. If it be intelligent, brave, and pure, it is because the people demand these high qualities to represent them in the national legislature … If the next centennial does not find this a great nation … it will be because those who represent the enterprise, the culture and the morality of the nation do not aid in controlling the political forces."[47]

One of the simplest solutions for returning our nation to its original foundation is changing those in public office. This, however, will never occur as long as the church is inactive at the polls. Unfortunately, less than five percent of evangelical Americans are involved in party politics at the local level.

In elections, a candidate's party affiliation should not be the deciding factor. We need to investigate the position of each individual candidate, apart from his or her party, and then make our choices before we vote.

The enemy is not "them." The enemy is "inactivity." While complacency rules, wrong principles and policies will abound. We must be involved if we are to recover our roots. Our Founding Fathers did their part. They gave us a Constitution for the ages. Now it is up to us to do everything we can to keep it. Some Christians feel like they are forced to stay at the back of the bus and are only allowed to go into a tiny little corner. Some Christians feel that they are a persecuted minority in a nation that they founded.[48] In reality we have a great opportunity, like there have been few opportunities before, to make a real difference in the lives of people across the country. It is our duty and obligation as men and women serving Christ to go out and make that difference. Ralph Waldo Emerson said:

We need to get out and vote!

"The greatness of a nation is not ultimately measured in its senses or in its population. The greatness of a nation is not measured in the abundance of its national resources or in the wealth of its crops. The true greatness of a nation is measured by the kind of men and women it produces."[49]

Page four of the U.S. Constitution bears the words: "in the year of our Lord," referring to Jesus Christ.

By that measure, America has produced persons of true greatness such as Washington, Jefferson, Lincoln, Webster, and Roosevelt. We need to produce more of them in this day and age. There may be a tendency to become discouraged due to the toughness of the battle because we have reaped what we have sown. God has given us a choice to either reap His blessings or reap His curses. Today we are reaping the inevitable results of our rejection of God. It is time to take America back!

This then, is our moment in history. Decades may pass before another generation has the opportunity to effect change in this magnitude. We need to leave the comfort of our families, churches, and communities, and take a risk. This is the challenge of our day. Will history condemn us for allowing our moment to pass without a resolute commitment to make a difference in the future due to our apathy and self-indulgence? Our nation is at a crossroad and what we do now could affect the next century of American history.

Greatest Opportunity[50]

"War must be carried on systematically and to do it, you must have men of character activated by principles of honor." —*General George Washington (1732-1799)*

Many Christians search their entire lives for a chance at greatness because they misunderstand the dynamics of Christ's kingdom. At first, you may dream of becoming the next Bill Gates or the President of the United States. Eventually, you settle on more realistic goals, such as becoming involved in a political campaign, joining a church, or setting money aside for your retirement or for your children's education. Whatever the goal, it is important for you to define your life goals and embrace a sense of purpose.

But what about the specific role God has given you, at your home address, so to speak, on the broad highway of humanity? Finding and fulfilling one's personal destiny is every person's highest goal, the sphere of your God-given calling. Enter a zone of maximum impact by changing how you view and respond to the world around you.

We often try many different things before we understand the specific calling that the Lord has for us. If we are wise enough to develop our character and unique giftings, we will eventually be able to function in an area with greatness and experience true fulfillment. But great teams are not just the result of individual superstars. God has pre-wired us with natural talents and loaded us with brilliant software called "gifts of the Spirit" that help us to function together.

Along with our gifts, training and discipline are crucial to success. When it comes to taking up the torch for our country and finding specific goals we are called to reach, we must be prepared, educated, and willing to make a difference. Our strategies have to include either occupying or electing dedicated Christians to occupy critical posts in poli-

Lady Liberty weeps for our nation.

tics and law. We can become a world-class warrior, but it demands a lifestyle based upon discipline, commitment, and the Word of God.

It is easy to look at our nation's rich Christian heritage and the extent of our spiritual and moral decline and feel overwhelmed by the massive rebuilding effort that will be required to restore America's foundations. The temptation is to surrender to the seeming hopelessness of the task and to sit back and do nothing. And that is exactly what we must not do. The need is for each of us to do *something*. We need to begin *now* the process of becoming better informed and involved as a part of the solution.

You and I are writing the script of America's future today. With every word, every decision, every thought, every act—for good or ill—we are either rebuilding our foundations or bringing further decay. Each one of us plays a part and bears the consequences. History is now rolling up like a scroll, and we must reassess our moments of destiny. Did we, as a nation, recognize and respond to the divine hand in history? Did you and I grasp the moment of grace extended to us?

> "God is going to reveal to us things He never revealed before if we put our hands in His. No books ever go into my laboratory. The thing I am to do and the way of doing it are revealed to me. I never have to grope for methods. The method is revealed to me the moment I am inspired to create something new. Without God to draw aside the curtain, I would be helpless." —*George Washington Carver*

This is the greatest opportunity that you and I have ever had personally to make a difference. I hope that you will begin today, if you have not already begun. The seriousness of our nation's dilemma will not permit delay. Every day is critical. Your life counts!

✠

Endnotes

Foreword

1. Don Wildmon, *American Family Association Journal,* Line 31, No. 3 (March 2007), p. 2.
2. Stephen McDowell, *Reformation Report,* Vol 16, No.1, p. 1.

PART ONE: THE PAST

Chapter 1

1. Writings of Christopher Columbus from his own journal, as quoted on *God's Mighty Hand: Providential Occurrences in World History,* by Richard Wheeler (Mantle Ministries Press: Bulverde, TX), pp. 41-43.
2. *The Log of Christopher Columbus,* translated by Robert H. Fuson (International Marine Publishing: Camden, Maine) (Hamilton Printing Company: Rensselaer, NY), p. 187.
3. Ibid., pp. 132-133.
4. Ibid., p. 149.
5. Ibid, p. 196.
6. Rousas J. Rushdoony, *This Independent Republic: Studies in the Nature and Meaning of American History* (Nutley, NJ: The Craig Press, 1964), pp. 97-98.
7. Jon Meacham, *American Gospel,* (Random House: New York, 2006), p. 42.
8. John Smith, "The Starving Time in Virginia," in Richard Dorson, ed., *America Begins: Early American Writings* (New York: Pantheon, 1950), pp. 138-142; Alden Vaughan, *American Genesis: Captain John Smith and the Founding of Virginia* (Boston: Little Brown, 1975).
9. Nathanial Philbrick, *The Mayflower* (Penguin Group: New York, 2006), p. 6.
10. This account is drawn from several sources, including Bernard Bailyn et al., *The Great Republic: A History of the American People* (Lexington, MA: February 13, 2004, C. Heath, 1992), pp. 44-45; Clarence Ver Steeg, *The Informative Years: 1607-1763* (New York: Hill and Wang, 1964), pp. 26-27.
11. Robert A. Divine, T. H. Breen, George M. Fredrickson, R. Hal Williams, *The American Story* (Addison-Wesley Educational Publisher's Inc., New York, NY), pp. 53-54.
12. Ibid., p. 55.
13. Ibid.
14. "Fundamental Orders of Connecticut" (January 14, 1629), Documents, 23.
15. "The New England Confederation" (May 19, 1643), Documents, 26.
16. Expanded version of this historical material can be found in Gary DeMar's *America's Christian History: The Untold Story, 2nd ed.* (Powder Springs, GA: American Vision, 1995); *America's Christian Heritage* (Nashville, TN: Broadman & Holman, 2003); Gary DeMar, *Building a City on a Hill* (Powder Springfield, GA: American Vision, 2005).
17. Gordon Wood, "The Radical Revolution: An Interview with Gordon Wood," interview by Fredric Smoler, *American Heritage* (December 1992), p. 52.
18. Steven Morris, "America's Unchristian Beginnings," *The Los Angeles Times* (August 3, 1995), p. B-9.
19. Michael A. MacDonald, "Founding Fathers Weren't Devout," *The Charlotte Observer* (January 15, 1993), p. 7A.
20. Isaac Kramnick and R. Laurence Moore, *The Godless Constitution, The Case Against Religious Correctness* (New York: W.W. Norton & Company, 1996).
21. M. Stanton Evans "Faith of our Fathers," *The American Spectator*, Volume 40, Number 1 (February 2007), pp. 22-27.
22. Zachary Karabell, *A Visionary Nation: Four Centuries of American Dreams and What Lies Ahead* (New York: Harper Collins Publishers, 2001), pp. 8-9.

Chapter 2

1.   Nathaniel Philbrick, *The Mayflower* (Penguin Group: New York, 2006), p. 6.

2.   Accounts of various laws come from Thomas Jefferson Wertenbaker, *The Puritan Oligarchy: The Founding of American Civilization* (New York: Grosset & Dunlap, 1947), pp. 172ff. Also, Edmund Morgan, *Visible Saints: The History of a Puritan Idea* (Ithaca: Cornell University Press, 1963).

3.   Quoted in Perry Miller, *Errand into the Wilderness* (Cambridge: Harvard University Press, 1984), p. 11.

4.   Edward Johnson, J. F. Jameson, ed., *Wonder-Working Providence 1628-1652* (New York, 1910), pp. 55-85; Increase Mather, "The Mystery of Israel's Salvation" (1667)), in Alam Heimart and Andrew Delbanco, eds., *The Puritans in America: A Narrative Anthology* (Cambridge: Harvard University Press, 1985), pp. 237-46; John Winthrop, "A Model of Christian Charity 1630," in Edwin Gaustad, ed., *A Documentary History of Religion in America to the Civil War* (Grand Rapids, MI: Eerdmans, 1982), pp. 106-107. Also, Philip Gura, *A Glimpse of Sion's Glory* (Middleton, Conn.: Wesleyan University Press, 1984).

5.   William J. Murray, *The Pledge: One Nation Under God* (Living Ink Books, Chattanooga, TN: 2007), p. 103.

6.   Larry Schweikart and Michael Allen, *A Patriot's History of the United States* (Penguin Group, New York, 2004), p. 26.

7.   Francis D. Cogliano, *Revolutionary America (1763-1815)* (Routledge Press, New York, NY, 2003), p. 25.

8.   William Bradford, *Of Plymouth Plantation, 1650*; Harold Paget, ed., *Bradford's History of the Plymouth Settlement 1650-1680* (San Antonio: Mantle Ministries, 1988. Paget's original version published 1909), p. 21.

9.   D. James Kennedy and Jerry Newcombe, "What if America were a Christian Nation Again?" (Nashville, TN: Thomas Nelson, Inc., 2003), pp. 20-21.

10.   Church of Holy Trinity v. U.S. 143 US 457 (1892).

11.   Paul Johnson, *A History of the American* (New York: Harper Collins Publishers, 1997), p. 28.

12.   Bancroft, *History of the United States of America*, Vol. 1, p. 207.

13.   Lillback Proclaim Liberty, pp. 84-86; Sanford H. Cobb, *The Rise of Religious Liberty in America* (New York: Macmillan Co., 1902), p. 419; Peter A. Lillback "Wall of Misconception" (Providence Forum Press: West Conshohocken, PA, 2007), p. 166.

14.   George Washington, "The Writings of George Washington from the Original Manuscript Sources: 1749-1799," John C. Fitzpatrick (Washington, DC: United States Government Printing Office, 1936), 15:55.

15.   George Washington, *Proclamation: A National Thanksgiving, A Compilation of the Messages and Papers of the Presidents, 1789-1902*, John D. Richardson, 11 Volumes (Washington, DC: Bureau of Natural Literature Art, 1907), pp. 1-64.

16.   Richard B. Morris, *Encyclopedia of American History* (New York: Harper and Row Publisher, 1953), p. 128.

17.   William J. Federer, *The Ten Commandments and their Influence on American Law* (St. Louis, MO: Amerisearch, Inc., 2003), p. 216.

18.   Evans, pp. 22-27.

19.   Michael and Janna Novak, "Washington's God" as quoted in *The Washington Times* (April 9, 2006), p. 22.

20.   D. James Kennedy and Jerry Newcombe, *Lord of All: Developing a Christian World and Life View* (Crossway Books: Wheaton, Illinois, 2006), p. 123.

21.   Evans, pp. 22-27.

22.   William J. Federer, *3 Secular Reasons Why America Should Be Under God* (Amerisearch, Inc.: St. Louis, 2004), p. 36.

23. Bryan Curtis, *A Call for Freedom* (Rutledge Hill Press, Nashville, Tennessee), p. 80.

24. Dr. D. James Kennedy, *The Declaration of Independence and the Constitution of the United States of America* (Coral Ridge Ministried, Ft. Lauderdale, FL: 2004), pp. 3-6.

25. Evans, pp. 22-27.

26. Ibid.

27. Samuel Adams, *The Writings of Samuel Adams*, Harry Alonzo Cushing, editor (New York: G. P. Putnam's Sons, 1907), Vol. IV, p. 256, in the Bostom Gazette on April 16, 1781.

28. Gorton Caruth and Eugene Ehrlich, ed., *American Quotations* (Wing Books: Avenil, NJ, 1992), p. 107.

29. Charles Crismier, *Renewing the Soul of America* (Elijah Books: Richmond, VA, 2002), p. 251.

30. The Declaration of Independence has five references to God: God as Creator of all men; God as the source of all hope; God as the supreme lawmaker; God as the very supreme judge; and God as our patron and protector. The Declaration proclaims God's existence as a self-evident truth, which requires no further discussion or debate.

Chapter 3

1. Thomas Jefferson to Benjamin Rush (April 21, 1803), Quoted in Gaustad, "Neither King Nor Prelate," p. 100.

2. Ibid.

3. Ibid. p. 101.

4. Mark A. Beliles's Introduction to an updated version of Thomas Jefferson's *Abridgement of the Words of Jesus of Nazareth* (Charlottesville, VA: The Providence Foundation, 1993), p. 7.

5. Thomas Jefferson to William Canby, 18 September 1813, Writings, XIII:377. Quoted in Harsberger, ed., *Treasury of Presidential Quotations*, p. 194.

6. Beliles, p. 103.

7. Theologically it's flawed to try to teach only the ethics and teachings of Jesus by removing the miracles. Nonetheless, Jefferson's approach was a far cry from the skeptical, anti-Christian tract that skeptics make the Jefferson Bible out to be.

8. Richard Peters, *The Public Statutes at Large of the United States of America, Vol VII* (Boston: Charles C. Little and James Brown, 1848), pp. 78-79.

9. American State Papers, Class VIII, Public Lands, Vol. III, Documents legislative and Executive, of the Congress of the United States, op. cit., 17th Congress, 2nd Session, Document N. 374, "Application of the United Brethren to Be Divested of the Trust Estate of the Lands Conveyed for the Benefit of Certain Christian Indians," p. 714.

10. Beliles, p. 103.

11. He wanted to bring the entire faculty of Calvin's theological seminary over from Geneva, Switzerland, and establish them at the University of Virginia.

12. Gary DeMar, *Biblical World View*, Volume 20, No. 6 (June, 2004), p. 3.

13. A letter to John Adams in 1813, quoted in Douglas Lurton's, "Foreward," *The Jefferson Bible* (Cleveland, OH: The World Publishing Co., 1942), p. ix.

14. Ferrara, Religion and the Constitution, p. 34-35. For a comprehensive study of the historical meaning of the separation of church and state, see Philip Hamburger, *Separation of Church and State* (Cambridge, MA: Harvard University Press, 2002).

15. Letter from Thomas Jefferson to Bishop Carroll (September 3, 1801) (Library of Congress, Number 19), p. 966.

16. 11 Annals of Congress 1, 332 (1802); 12 Annals of Congress 1, 602 (1803); 12 Annals of Congress 1, 279 (1804).

17. Letter from Thomas Jefferson to the Nuns of the Order of St. Ursula (New Orleans, LA: May 25, 1804).
18. Letter from Thomas Jefferson to Dr. Thomas Cooper (November 2, 1822).
19. David Barton, *The Founding Father and Deism* (Wall Builders, 2002).
20. Edwin S. Gusted, *Neither King Nor Prelate: Religion and the New Nation, 1776-1826, rev. ed.* (Grand Rapids: MI: Erdmann (1787) 1993), p. 100.
21. Garry Wills, *Under God: Religion and American Politics* (New York: Simon and Schuster, 1990), pp. 354-355.
22. David Barton, "The Image and the Reality: Thomas Jefferson and the First Amendment," Notre Dame Law School, Volume Seventeen (2003), p. 431.
23. Letter from Thomas Jefferson to the Reverend Samuel Miller, 23 January, 1808, The Writings of Thomas Jefferson, ed. Andrew A Lipscomb and Albert Ellery Bergh, 20 vols. (Washington DC: Thomas Jefferson Memorial Association, 1905), 11:428.
24. Stephen Marshfield, *Ten Tortured Words* (Thomas Nelson Publishers, Nashville, TN 2007), p. 146; Thomas Jefferson, Notes on Virginia, (Query XVIII, 1781, 1782), p. 237.
25. Scholars believe that, as a result of reading sometime around 1793, Joseph Priestley's *An History of the Corruptions of Christianity,* Jefferson experienced a "conversion" to Unitarian Christianity. Priestley's book persuaded Jefferson that he was a Christian after all and henceforth he was not reluctant to proclaim the fact to his friends. Hames H. Hutson, *Religion and the Founding of the American Republic* (The Library of Congress: Washington DC, 1998), p. 83.

Chapter 4

1. Perry Miller, *Religion in Society in the Early Literature of Virginia* (Cambridge, MA, 1956), p. 175.
2. Matthew D. Staver, Liberty Counsel.
3. Benjamin Ruth, Essays, p. 8., "Of the Mode of Education Proper in a Republic."
4. David Barton, *The Role of Pastors and Christians in Civil Government* (Aleda, TX: Wall Builder Press, 2003). p. 22.
5. Stephen Mansfield, *Ten Tortured Words* (Thomas Nelson Publishers, Nashville, TN 2007), p. 144; To the Officers of the First Brigade of the 3rd Division of the Massachusetts Militia, October 11, 1789. Adams Papers, Microfilm Reed, 119 Library of Congress.
6. Patricia U. Bonomi, *Under the Cope of Heaven: Religion, Society and Politics in Colonial America* (New York, 1986), p. 267.
7. D. James Kennedy and Jerry Newcombe, *What if America were a Christian Nation Again?* (Nashville, TN: Thomas Nelson, Inc., 2003), p. 32.
8. Samuel Adams, "The Rights of the Colonists," 1772, The Annals of America, Vol. 2, pp. 218-219.
9. John Adams, Letter to Thomas Jefferson, 25 December 1813, Correspondence, II, 412 quoted in Harnsberger, Ed., Treasury of Presidential Quotations, p. 211. Quoted in Ibid, p. 116.
10. Benjamin Rush, Essays, *Literary, Moral and Philosophical* (1798, 2nd edition, 1806) quoted in Stephen Abbot Northrop, A Cloud of Witnesses (Portland, OR: American Heritage Ministries, 1987), p. 388.
11. The Adams-Jefferson Letters, UNC Press 1959, Vol. 2, p. 412; Reprinted in Federer, America's God and Country Encyclopedia of Quotations, p. 13.
12. Patrick Henry of Virginia, Plymouth Rock Foundation, Marlborough, NH, p. iii; Reprinted in Federer, America's God and Country Encyclopedia of Quotations, p. 289.
13. Ibid., p. 574.
14. David Limbaugh, *Persecution: How Liberals are Waging War Against Christianity* (New York: Perennial Press, 2004), p. 320.
15. Benjamin Rush, "Essays, Literary, Moral and Philosophical (Philadelphia: Thomas and Samuel F.

Bradford, 1798), p. 8, "Of the Mode of Education Proper in a Republic;" See also, Rush, Letters, Vol. II, pp. 820-821, to Thomas Jefferson on August 22, 1800, and Rush, Essays, pp. 112-113, "Defense of the Use of the Bible as a School Book."

Chapter 5

1. Marsh v. Chambers, 463 U.S. 783 (1983).
2. See, for example, Steven K. Green, "Federalism and the Establishment Clause: A Reassessment," 38 CREIGHTON L. REV. 761, 769 (2005) (stating that six or seven states maintained religious establishments when the First Amendment was ratified).
3. E.g., CONN. CONST. art VII; GA. CONST. Art. III, § 4, para. IV: VT. CONST. art. III; N.H. CONST. art. V.
4. Green, supra note 80.
5. U.S. CONST. art. I § 2, cl. 1 (emphasis added).
6. See id.
7. Scott C. Idleman, "Liberty in the Balance: Religion, Politics, and American Constitutionalism," 71 NOTRE DAME L. REV., 991, 995 (1996); See, for example, DAVIS V. BEASON.
8. U.S. CONST. art. VI, cl. 3.
9. Id.
10. Jeffrey J. Ventrella, "The Cathedral Builder –Pursuing Cultural Beauty" (American Vision, Powder Springs, GA. 1007), pp. 242-243.
11. See Orthodox Presbyterian Church, supra note 93; "Orthodox Presbyterian Church," LARGER CATE-CHISM 115 – 121: http://www.opc.org/lc.html (last visited June 10, 2006).
12. THE SHORTER OXFORD ENGLISH DICTIONARY 2642 (5th ed. 2002) (defining Sabbatarian as "[a] Christian who [strictly] observes the [Sunday] Sabbath."); see, for example, supra note 96, ch. XXI; "Orthodox Presbyterian Church," SHORTER CATECHISM 57 – 58: http://opc.org/sc.html (last visited June 10, 2006).
13. See, for example, U.S. CONST. art. I, § 7, cl. 2.
14. U.S. CONST. art. I, § 7, cl. 2 (emphasis added).
15. David Barton, CHURCH IN THE U.S. CAPITOL: http://wallbuilders.com/LIBissuesArticles.asp?id=90 (last visited June 10, 2006).
16. Id.
17. Daniel L. Dreisbach, THOMAS JEFFERSON AND THE WALL OF SEPARATION BETWEEN CHURCH AND STATE 21 – 22 (N.Y. Univ. Press 2002). The metaphor by Thomas Jefferson was written in 1802, two years after Congress approved having church services in the Capitol. Id. Two days later, Jefferson was worshipping in the Capitol. Id. Unless he is impugned for being a rank hypocrite, his private metaphor cold not mean what today's religious censors contend that it means. See also Philip Hamburger, SEPARATION OF CHURCH AND STATE 144 – 89 (Harvard Univ. Press 2002).
18. 6 ANNALS OF CONG. 787 (1800).
19. Jeffrey J. Ventrella, "The Cathedral Builder – Pursuing Cultural Beauty" (American Vision, Powder Springs, GA. 1007), p. 246.
20. Alexis de Tocqueville, "Democracy in America," Henry Reeve, Phillips Bradley (New York, 1945), I, 311.

Chapter 6

1. Benjamin Franklin, Papers, (1961), Vol. III, pp. 226-227. "Proclamation for a General Fast on December 9, 1747" (Franklin, Works (1840), Vol. I, pp. 148-149).
2. Remarks of Benjamin Franklin, May 14, 1787, National Constitution Convention, as quoted in *God's*

Mighty Hand: Providential Occurrences in World History, by Richard Wheeler (Bulverde, TX: Mantle Ministries Press), pp. 118-119.

3.   Benjamin Franklin, "Proposals Relating to the Education of Youth in Pennsylvania" (Philadelphia, 1749), p. 22.

4.   Benjamin Franklin, Letter to Ezra Stiles, March 9, 1790 EG39.

5.   Story, Joseph. 1833. Joseph Story, "Commentaries on the Constitution," 1833 (Boston: Hilliard, Gray & Co., 1833; reprinted NY: Da Capo Press, 1970), Vol. III, p. 726, Sec. 1868, & p. 727, Sec. 1869. Joseph Story, *A Familiar Exposition of the Constitution of the United States* (MA: Marsh, Capen Lyon & Webb, 1840; reprinted NY: Harper & Brothers, 1854; reprinted Washington, DC: Regnery Gateway, 1986), pp. 259-261, p. 314, Sec. 441, p. 316, Sec. 444. Joseph Story, "Commentaries on the Constitution of the United States" (1891), Secs. 1874, 1876, 1877.

6.   Joseph Story (1779-1845) was appointed by President James Madison to the U.S. Supreme Court. Madison was a key framer of the First Amendment. Story spent thirty-four years as a Supreme Court justice. During most of that time he was also the Dane Professor of Law at Harvard University, where he was greatly responsible for helping establish the law school's success and reputation. He authored the noted multi-volume set of books about the Constitution cited above.

7.   Ronald D. Rotunda and John E. Novak, eds., Joseph Story: "Commentaries on the Constitution of the United States" (Durham, NC; Carolina Academic Press, 1987), sec. 988, p. 700.

8.   Joseph Story: "Commentaries on the Constitution" 3:sec. 1867; http://press-pubs.uchicago.edu/founders/print_documents/amendI_religions69.html.

9.   Stephen Mansfield, *Ten Tortured Words* (Thomas Nelson Publishers: Nashville, TN 2007), p. 25.

10. Joseph Story, "Commentaries of the Constitution of the United States," 2nd ed., Vol. II (Charles C. Little and James Brown: Boston, 1851), sec. 1874, 593.

11. William J. Federer, *America's God and Country, Encyclopedia of Quotations* (Coppell, TX: Fame Publishing Co., 1994), p. 412.

12. Henry P. Johnston, *The Correspondence and Public Papers of John Jay* (New York: Burt Franklin, 1970), Vol. IV, p. 393.

13. Daniel Webster, "Esteemed as One of the Five Greatest Senators in U.S. History by Resolution of the United States Senate." *The Capitol: A Pictorial History of the Capitol and of Congress,* 8th Ed., House Document 96-376, 96th congress, p. 112.

14. Webster, Daniel. Benjamin Franklin Morse, *The Christian Life and Character of the Divil Institutions of the United States of America* (Philadelphia: George W. Childs, 1864), p. 270.

15. Sir William Blackstone, "Commentaries on the Laws of England," quoted in John Eidsmoe, *Christianity and the Constitution, the Faith of our Founding Fathers* (Grand Rapids, MI: Baker Books, 1987), p. 58.

16. David Barton, *Original Intent, The Courts, The Constitution and Religion* (Aledo, TX: Wallbuilder Press, 1996), p. 225.

17. Virginia Armstrong, Ph.D., is the President of the Blackstone Institute and National Chairman of Eagle Forum's Court Watch. She writes and speaks widely on the constitution, jurisprudence, and Christian apologetics. Rare Jewel Magazine, April 2005, pp. 31-33.

18. Donald S. Lutz, "The Relative Influence of European Writers on Late Eighteenth Century American Political Thought," American Political Science Review, Vol. 78 (1987), p. 184.

19. Gary DeMar, *America's Christian History: The Untold Story* (Atlanta, GA: American Vision, Inc., 1993), p. 133.

20. Alexis de Tocqueville, Robert N. Bellah, *Habits of the Heart, The Biblical World View* (Atlanta, GA: Am American Vision Publication, 1993), Vol 9, No. 2, p. 14.

21. Alexis de Tocqueville, *The Republic of the United States and Its Political Institutions Reviewed and Examined, Volume I*, translated Henry Reeves (A.S. Barnes and Co.: Garden City, NY, 1851), p. 335.

22. Abraham Lincoln, "Selected Speeches, Messages and Letters," T. Harry Williams (New York 1957), p. vi.

23. Richard V. Pierard and Robert D. Linder, "Civil Religion and the Presidency" (Grand Rapids: Academia e.i. books, 1988), pp. 11-64.

24. Abraham Lincoln, March 30, 1863, in a Proclamation of a National Day of Humiliation, Fasting and Prayer. James D Richardson (U.S. Representative-TN), ed., "A Compilation of the Messages and Papers of the Presidents," 1789-1897, 10 Vols. (Washington, DC: U.S. Government Printing Office, published by Authority of Congress, 1897, 1899; Washington, DC: Bureau of National Literature & Art, 1789-1902, 11 Vols., 1907, 1910), Vol. VI, pp. 164-165. Roy Basler, ed., *Collected Works of Abraham Lincoln* (Rutgers Univ. Press, 1953), Vol. 6, p. 179. Benjamin Weiss, *God in American History: A Documentation of America's Religious Heritage* (Grand Rapids, MI: Zondervan, 1966), p. 92.

25. Abraham Lincoln, July 15, 1863, National Day of Thanksgiving, Praise & Prayer Proclamation. James D. Richardson (U.S. Representative-TN), ed., "A Compilation of the Messages & Papers of the Presidents," 1789-1897, 10 Vols. (Washington DC: U.S. Government Printing Office, published by Authority of Congress, 1897, 1899; Washington, DC: Bureau of National Literature & Art, 1789-1902, 11 Vols., 1907, 1010), Vol. 6, p. 170.

26. Elias Boudinot, "The Life, Public Services, Addresses, and Letters of Elias Boudinot, L.L.C., President of the Continental Congress," J.J. Boudinot, editor (Boston: Houghton, Mifflin and Co., 1896), Vol. I, pp. 19, 21, speech in the First Provincial Congress of New Jersey.

27. Bernard C. Steiner, "The Life and Correspondence of James McHenry" (Cleveland: The Burrows Brothers, 1907), p. 475, to James McHenry on November 4, 1800.

28. *Independent Chronicle* (Boston: November 2, 1780), last page; see also Abram English Brown, "John Hancock, His book" (Boston: Lee and Shepard, 1898), p. 269.

29. Benjamin Rush, "Essays, Literary, Moral and Philosophical" (Philadelphia: Thomas and Samuel F. Bradford, 1798), p. 8, "Of the Mode of Education Proper in a Republic;" See also, Rush, Letters, Vol. II, pp. 820-821, to Thomas Jefferson on August 22, 1800, and Rush, Essays, pp. 112-113, "Defense of the Use of the Bible as a School Book."

30. Stephen Hopkins, "The Rights of the Colonies Examined" (Providence: William Goddard, 1765), pp. 23-24.

31. Wells, "Life and Services of Samuel Adams," Vol. III, pp. 372-373, to Thomas Paine on November 30, 1802; see Also Vol. I, p. 504, and Samuel Adams and John Adams, "Four Letters: Being an Interesting Correspondence Between Those Eminently Distinguished Characters, John Adams, Late President of the United States; and Samuel Adams, Late Governor of Massachusetts, on the Important Subject of Government" (Boston: Adams and Rhoades, 1802), pp. 9-10.

32. Washington, Writings (1936), Vol. XV, p. 55, from his speech to the Delaware Indian Chiefs on May 12, 1779; see also Washington, Writings (1932), Vol. V, pp. 244-245, July 9, 1776 (this statement of George Washington was also used by Abraham Lincoln in his November 15, 1862, order to his troops to maintain regular Sabbath observances); see Abraham Lincoln, "Letters and Addresses of Abraham Lincoln," Mary MacLean, editor (New York: Unit Book Publishing Co., 1907), p. 261; see also Washington, Writings, Vol. II, pp. 342-343, General Orders of May 2, 1778.

33. Alexander Hamilton, "The Papers of Alexander Hamilton," Harold C. Syrett, editor (New York: Columbia University Press, 1977), Vol. XXV, pp. 605-610, to James Bayard on April 16-21, 1802.

34. "Reports of the Proceedings and Debates of the Convention of 1821," Assembled for the Purpose of Amending the Constitution of the State of New York (Albany: E. And E. Hosford, 1821), p. 575, Rufus King, October 30, 1821.

35. John Dickinson, "The Political Writings of John Dickinson" (Wilmington: Bonsal and Niles, 1801), Vol. I, p. 111.

36. "The Debates and Proceedings in the Congress of the United States" (Washington: Gales and Seaton, 1834), Vol. I, pp. 949-950, September 25, 1789.
37. M'Creery's Lessee v. Alender, 4 Harris & McHenry 258, 259 (Sup. Ct. Md. 1799), where Justice Samuel Chase applied a belief in Christianity as the basis of citizenship in the case.

PART TWO: THE PRESENT
Chapter 7
1. Daniel Webster, from a discourse delivered at Plymouth, December 22, 1820.
2. Witherspoon, Works, III:42, from "The Dominion of Providence Over the Passions of Men," delivered at Princeton on May 17, 1776.
3. William DeLoss Love, Jr., *The Fast and Thanksgiving Days of New England*, (Houghton Mifflin Publishing Co., Cambridge, 1895); *Proclamation of Thanksgiving, With an Historical Introduction and Notes* (Munsell and Rowland Co., Albany, 185); HSJ Sickel, *Thanksgiving; In Source, Philosophy, and History* (Philadelphia International Printing Co., Philadelphia, 1940).
4. William Bradford, *Of Plymouth Plantation*, (The Modern Library, New York, 1952), p. 90.
5. Dianna Karter Appelbaum, *Thanksgiving: An American Holiday, An American History* (New York: Facts on File Publications, 1984), p. 14.
6. Paul C. Vitz, *Censorship: Evidence of Bias in Our Children's Textbooks* (Ann Arbor, MI: Servant Books, 1986).
7. D. James Kennedy, *Restoring the Real Meaning of Thanksgiving* (Coral Ridge Ministries, Ft. Lauderdale, FL., 1989). Charles Hull Wolfe, "The Threat to Thanksgiving Day," *The Coral Ridge Encounter Magazine* (November 1988), p. 3.
8. *Glassroth v. Moore*, 242 F. Supp. 2d 1067 (2002).
9. "Court Says Monument Violates Constitution," *Southern Poverty Law Center Report* (December 2002), Volume 32, Number 4.
10. *Stone v. Graham*, 449 U.S. 39, 42 (1980).
11. Gary DeMar, "Mount Rushmore and the Christian Entablature," *The Biblical Worldview* (September 2003), pp. 19-20.
12. Benjamin Weiss, *God in American Histoy: A Documentation of America's Religious Heritage* (Zondervan: Grand Rapids, MI, 1966), pp. 208-224.
13. Roy Moore, *So Help Me God* (Broadman and Holman Publishers: Nashville, TN, 2005), p. 45.
14. Jon Meacham, *American Gospel* (Random House: NY, 2006), p. 81; Edwin S. Gaustad, *Proclaim Liberty throughout All the Land; A History of Church and State in America* (Oxford University Press; NY, [1999] 2003), ix-xi; For more information on the topic of the role Christianity played in the founding of America, see Gary DeMar, *America's Christian History: The Untold Story, 2nd ed.* (American Vision: Powder Springs, GA, 1995) and Gary DeMar, *America's Christian Heritage* (Broadman & Holman, Nashville, TN, 2003).

Chapter 8
1. Pat Robertson, *The Turning Tide* (Word Publishing: Dallas, TX, 1993), p. 262.
2. William J. Bennett, *The Broken Hearth* (Doubleday: NY, 2001), p. 10.
3. Paula Ettelbrick, "Since When Is Marriage a Path to Liberation?" OUT/LOOK, reprinted in Lesbians, Gay men, and the Law, ed. Wm. Rubenstein (Fall 1989), pp. 402, 403, 405; Jeffrey J. Ventrella, *The Cathedral Builder—Pursuing Cultural Beauty* (American Vision: Powder Springs, GA, 1007), p. 216.
4. Paul C. Vitz, *Censorship: Evidence of Bias in Our Children's Textbooks* (Ann Arbor, MI: Servant Books, 1986), p. 1.

5.   For a list of sources, see Richard F. Duncan, *Public Schools and the Inevitability of Religious Inequality,* 1996, byul rev. 569 Note 45: Gilbert T. Sewall, Religion and the Textbooks, Curriculum, Religion and Public Education 79 (1998).

6.   Dianna Karter Appelbaum, *Thanksgiving: An American Holiday, An American History* (New York: Facts on File Publications, 1984), p. 9.

7.   Vitz.

8.   Ibid.

9.   Information in this article was taken from *Restoring America's Christian Education* by Stephen McDowell, Providence Foundation, "Enjoying Everyday Life," July, 2004, pp. 10-11 (The Providence Foundation: Charlottesville, VA, 2000), www.providencefoundation.com

10. John H. Westerhoff III, *The Struggle For A Common Culture: Biblical Images in 19th Century Schoolbooks* (Philadelphia, PA: Fortress Press, 1982), p. 32.

11. ACLU.

12. ACLU.

13. Peggy Lamson, *Roger Baldwin: Founder of the ACLU: A Portrait* (Boston: Houglon-Mifflin, 1976), p. 192.

14. "1992 Policy Guide of the ACLU," policy 4d, p. 7 and policy 4g, p. 9; Alan Sears and Craig Osten, *The ACLU vs. America* (Nashville, TN: Broadman & Holman Publishers, 2005), p. 3.

15. Ibid., policy 4e, p. 8.

16. "ACLU Defends Library against Parent Seeking Internet Censorship," ACLU of Northern California press release, October 19, 1999; http://www.aclunc.org/news/press_releases/aclu_in_court_again_to_defend_library_against_ca_parent _seeking_internet_censorship_shtml?ht2, and "ACLU Defends California Library against Parent Seeking to Compel Internet Censorship," ACLU press release, July 10,1998 http://www.aclunc.org/news/press_releases/aclu_defends_ca_library_against_parent_seeking_to_ compel_internet_censorship.shtml?ht=; Alan Sears and Craig Osten, *The ACLU vs. America* (Nashville, TN; Broadman & Holman Publishers, 2005), p. 3.

17. "1992 Policy Guide of the ACLU," policy 2a, p. 3; Alan Sears and Craig Osten, *The ACLU vs. America* (Nashville, TN: Broadman & Holman Publishers, 2005), p. 3.

18. "Ban on Gays in the Military Goes on Trial: 'Don't Ask, Don't Tell,' Faces Challenge in Brooklyn," ACLU press release, March 12, 1995; http://archive.aclu.org/news/n031295c.html; Alan Sears and Craig Osten, *The ACLU vs. America* (Nashville, TN: Broadman & Holman Publishers, 2005), p. 3.

19. "1992 Policy Guide of the ACLU," policy 62a, p. 120, and policy 86, p. 168; Alan Sears and Craig Osten, *The ACLU vs. America* (Nashville, TN: Broadman & Holman Publishers, 2005), p. 3.

20. Ibid., policy 81, p. 161.

21. Ibid., policy 88, p. 171, and policy 89, p. 172.

22. Ibid., policy 91a, p. 175.

23. Adrain Brune, "ACLU Takes Center Stage in Gay Marriage Debate," Washington Blade, April 16, 2004; Alan Sears and Craig Osten, The ACLU vs. America (Nashville, TN: Broadman & Holman Publishers, 2005), p. 3.

24. Nada Mourtada-Sabbah, "Adopting 'In God We Trust' as the U.S. national motto, "Journal of Church and State (September 2002), http://findarticles.com/p/articles/mi_hb3244/is_200209/ai_n7953651.

25. William J. Murray, *The Pledge: One Nation Under God* (Chattanooga, TN: Living Ink Books, 2007), p. 87.

Chapter 9

1. *Everson v. Board of Education of Township of Ewing*, in County of Mercer, 330 U.S. 855 (1947).
2. The phrase "wall of separation" entered the lexicon of American constitutional law in the U.S. Supreme court's ruling in Reynolds vs. United States (1979). Most scholars agree that the wall metaphor played no role in the Court's decision. Alan Sears and Craig Osten, *The ACLU vs. America*, pp. 212-213.
3. *Vidal v. Girard*, 43 U.S. 127 (1844).
4. Anita Vogel, "Calif. Offers Textbook Case of Political Correctness," Fox News, April 30, 2003. Lawrence Morahan, "Psychiatric Association Debates Lifting Pedophilia Taboo," CNN News.com, June 11, 2002; John W. Whitehead, "The Rights of Religious Persons in Public Education: The Complete Resource for Knowing and Exercising Your Rights in Public Education" (Wheaton, IL: Crossway Books, 1991), p. 112.
5. "United Way in Dade Ends Boy Scout Funding," *The Miami Herald* (May 14, 2003).
6. "Pro-infanticide professor awarded ethics prize," *WorldNetDaily.com* (July 12, 2003).
7. Leo Pfeffer, *Church, State and Freedom* (Boston, MA: Beacon Press, 1953), p. 98.
8. *Lemon v. Kurtzman*, 403 U.S. 602 (1971).
9. M. Stanton Evans, *The Theme Is Freedom, Religion, Politics, and the American Tradition* (Washington DC: Regnery Publishing, Inc., 1994), p. 275.
10. "Montesquieu, *The Spirit of Laws* (New York: Hafner, 1949), quoted by John Eidsmoe, *Christianity in the Constitution, the Faith of Our Founding Fathers* (Grand Rapids, MI: Baker Books, 1987), p. 55.
11. Former U.S. Senator Zell Miller, "Deficit of Decency Speech" to U.S. Senate (2005).
12. George Goldberg, Church, *State and the Constitution, the Religion Clauses Upside Down* (Washington, DC: Regnery Gateway 1984), p. 11.
13. Pew Research Center Survey, March 10, 2002, "2002 Religion and Public Life Survey."
14. John M. Taylor, *Garfield of Ohio: The Available Man* (New York: W. W. Norton & Co., Inc., 1970), p. 180, quoted from "A Century of Congress" by James A. Garfield, *Atlantic*, July 1877.
15. John F. Kennedy, Inaugural Address, January 20, 1961, quoted on Caroline Thomas Harnsberger, ed., *Treasury of Presidential Quotations* (Follett: Chicago, 1964). D. James Kennedy and Jerry Newcombe, *Lord of All: Developing a Christian World and Life View* (Crossway Books: Wheaton, IL, 2006), p. 145.
16. Bob Dole, *Great Political Wit* (Doubleday: New York, New York, 1998), p. 119.

PART THREE: THE FUTURE

Chapter 10

1. Gary DeMar, *America's Christian Heritage* (Nashville, TN: Broadman and Holman Publishers, 2003), p. 85.
2. Dr. Edward Hindson, *National Liberty Journal,* Vol. 33, No. 6 (July 2004), p.6.
3 Gary DeMar, *Thinking Straight in a Crooked World* (American Vision, Inc., Powder Springs, GA, 1995), p. 11.
4. Ibid., p. 13.
5. Pat Robertson, *The Ten Offenses* (Integrity Publishers, Nashville, p. ix., x).
6. D. James Kennedy and Jerry Newcombe, *Lord of All: Developing a Christian World and Life View* (Crossway Books: Wheaton, IL, 2006), p. 19.
7. Colson and Pearcey, *How Now Shall We Live?* D. James Kennedy and Jerry Newcombe, *Lord of All: Developing a Christian World and Life View* (Crossway Books: Wheaton, IL, 2006), p. 13.
8. Judge Robert L. Dierker, Jr., *The Tyranny of Tolerance* (Crown Forum: New York, 2006), p. 1.
9. Richard A. Viguerie, *Conservatives Betrayed* (Bonus Books, Los Angeles, CA 2006), p. 112.
10. John Eidsmoe, *Christianity and the Constitution* (Grand Rapids, MI: Baker Books, 1987), p. 407.
11. Ibid., p. 410.

12. Kenneth Woodard, "How the Bible Made America," *Newsweek* (December 27, 1982), p. 45; George Gallup, Jr., *The People's Religion: American Faith in the '90s* (New York: MacMillan, 1989), p. 60; Rousas J. Rushdoony, *The Institutes of Biblical Law* (Phillipsburg, NJ: The Craig Press, 1973), p. 17; Gary North, *Political Polytheism: The Myth of Pluralism* (Tyler, TX: Institute for Christian Economics, 1989), p. 158.

13. Eidsmoe, p. 410.

14. Crystal Paul-Laughinghouse, "Leader of the ACLU Talks on Agenda," *Yale Daily News* (January 19, 2005).

15. "ACLU Wants to Legalize Polygamy," *Christians and Society Today* (June 1990), p. 4.

16. Alan Sears and Craig Osten, *The ACLU vs. America* (Broadman and Holmes: Nashville, TN 2005), p. 45

17. Volume 1, p. 22, as cited in Robert Morey's "An Analysis of the Hadith," The Hadith, (Faith Defenders: Orange, CA).

18. Ibid.

19. Thomas Arnold, *Sermons on the Christian Life: Its Hopes, Its Fears, Its Close, Sixth Edition* (London: T. Fellowes, 1859), p. 324.

20. Michael S. Horton, *Beyond Culture Wars* (Moody Press: Chicago, 1994), p. 39.

21. Ibid., p. 107.

22. Erwin W. Lutzer, *Will America Be Given Another Chance?* (Moody Press: Chicago, 1993), p. 42.

23. William Wirt Henry, ed., *Patrick Henry: Life, Correspondence and Speeches* (New York: Charles Scribner's Sons, 1891), Vol. II, 631.

24. Thomas Arnold, *Sermons on the Christian Life: Its Hopes, Its Fears, Its Close, Sixth Edition* (London: T. Fellowes, 1859), p. 235.

25. Henry, p. 631.

26. Gary L. Bauer, *Our Hope, Our Dreams* (Focus on the Family Publishing: Colorado Springs, CO, 1996), pp. 3-5.

27. Remarks from Lynn Buzard, founding director of the Christian Legal Society, in D. James Kennedy, *The Constitution in Crisis*, Ft. Lauderdale, FL: Coral Ridge Ministries, September, 1987.

28. *Compton's Pictured Encyclopedia and Fact Index* (Chicago, IL: F. E. Compton Co., 1965), Vol. 15, p. 192.

29. Quoted in Paul Little, *Know What You Believe* (Wheaton, IL: Victor Books, 1987), p. 124.

30. Dr. Paul Vitz, Censorship: Evidence of Bias in Our Children's Textbooks (Ann Arbor, MI: Servant Books, 1986).

31. Ibid.

32. Ken Ham, *The Lie Evolution* (Master Books: Green Forest, AR, 1987), p. 19.

33. Ibid., pp. 20-21.

34. David Limbaugh, *Persecution: How Liberals Are Waging War Against Christianity* (Regnery Publishing, Washington, DC: 2003), p. XII

35. Ibid.

36. 370 U.S. 421 (1962).

37. 472 U.S. 38 (1985).

38. Joseph Farah, *Whistleblower Magazine*, Taking Marriage Back (April, 2004), Vol. 13, #4.

39. Elizabeth Ridenour, *It's Coming Back: National Council on Bible Curriculum in Public Schools* (Greensboro, NC 2007).

40. Michael Farris, *The Joshua Generation* (Broadman and Holman: Nashville, TN; 1960, pp. 18-19).

41. Farah, See f. 38.

42. The total Department of Education Appropriations for 2007 was almost $66 billion dollars. But the

total cost for education State, Federal, local and all other expenditures for 2007 was $584 billion dollars.
U.S. Department of Education, *2008 Budget Summary* (Appendix 3).

43. Ben Shapira, *Brain Washed* (WND Books: Thomas Nelson Publishers, Nashville, TN, 2004) front flap.

44. David Limbaugh, "How Secularism Is Attempting to Abolish the Truth in our Culture" (*American Family Association Journal*, Vol. 28, No. 6), pp. 14-15.

45. Stephen McDowell, *Restoring America's Christian Education* (Providence Foundation: Charlottesville, VA 2000). Used with permission. See www.providencefoundation.com

46. R H. Warfel, *Noah Webster, Schoolmaster to America* (NY: MacMillan Co., 1936), pp. 181-182.

47. David Barton, *The Myth of Separation* (Aleda, TX: WallBuilder Press, 1992), pp. 264-268.

48. David John Marley, *Pat Robertson—An American Life* (NY: Rowman and Littlefield Publishers, 2007).

49. Ralph Waldo Emerson (1803-1882) was originally a Unitarian minister and left the ministry to pursue a career in writing and public speaking. He became one of America's best known and loved 19th century figures. After the death of his young wife and two elder brothers, Emerson began to doubt his faith and in 1832, he resigned the ministry and spent the remainder of his life thinking, writing, and speaking. He held the belief that the natural world held spiritual truths and an optimistic view of the human spirit.

50. Ron Luce, *Battlecry for a Generation: The Fight to Save America's Youth* (Cook Communications Ministriess: Colorado Springs, CO), pp. 31-34. Also see www.parentstv.org; www.frc.org or www.clickz.com/stats/sectors/demographics

About the Author

Dee's strong sense of family and community are reflected in his career. He joined his father Homer D. Wampler, Jr. (1913-1999) in the private practice of law in 1973 in Springfield, Missouri. Dee attended Drury College and Northwestern University, and graduated from the University of Missouri-Columbia (B.S. 1962; J.D. 1965). After active duty in the Army, Wampler was elected as one of Greene County, Missouri's youngest prosecuting attorneys. He was awarded the title of Springfield's Outstanding Young Man and Missouri's Outstanding Young Man in recognition of his community contributions. Dee served as President of the Springfield Metropolitan Bar Association and on the Board of Bar Governors for the Missouri Bar Association.

Dee has prosecuted and defended a large number of major felony cases, with his high profile work featured nationally on *Good Morning America, The Today Show, Inside Edition, Unsolved Mysteries, The 700 Club, Primetime,* and *The O'Reilly Factor*. He is the senior partner with the Wampler and Passanise Law Firm.

In addition to his successful trial work, Dee is widely recognized for his writings. He has published two hundred articles in various professional legal and law enforcement journals and has written four books on Missouri criminal law, including *Defending Yourself Against Cops in Missouri and Other Strange Places.* He is a popular lecturer, explaining the trial of Christ, and is the author of *The Trial of Christ: A Twentieth Century Lawyer Defends Jesus* and *The Myth of the Separation Between Church and State.*

Although renowned as a criminal defense attorney and acclaimed as an author and lecturer, Dee Wampler is above all a family man. Dee and his wife Anne are the proud parents of two adult children, Allison and John. Anne is the author of multiple volumes of Christian poetry including, *Look Only to Me, The Father's Heart, Living Water, Gold From the Fire,* and *The Voice of My Beloved.* The Wampler's daughter, Allison, is a classical violinist, and John is in the ministry and works for a hunger relief agency.